A Life Just Like Mine

Donna is an excellent motivational speaker and writer. If *A Life Just Like Mine* doesn't motivate you to examine and accept your own life, nothing will. Captivating read.

—**Rick Reed,** author of the Jack Murphy series

Dr. Kincheloe writes with passion and compassion in a way that readers from broken relationships like hers will feel understood and encouraged. This powerful book will encourage and strengthen you so you can say with the author, "the life God gave me made me."

—**James Watkins,** award-winning author of
Praise the Lord and Pass the Prozac

Donna Kincheloe writes with clarity and passion. If you are living from a life of pain, you need *A Life Just Like Mine.*

—**Brandt Dodson,** author of the Colton Parker mystery series
and *The Sons of Jude*

Donna models compassion in her personal and professional life. She is dedicated to making a difference in the lives of others, which she has done as a nurse and now as an author. Her insight into living a passionate life is something we can all benefit from.

—**Jennifer Evans,** DNP, RN, NC-BC Interim Assistant Dean and
Associate Professor of Nursing in the College of Nursing
and Health Professions at the University of Southern Indiana

Dr. Donna Kincheloe demonstrates how the transactional nature of extreme mental and emotional adversity led to a dependence on God and built the resilience needed for a successful career in nursing.

—**Lois M. Stallings Welden,** DNP, RN, CNS,
author, Nurse Researcher

Dr. Donna D. Kincheloe

A
Life
Just Like
Mine

HOW GOD & NURSING
TURNED PAST PAIN
INTO PRESENT PEACE

NEW YORK

LONDON • NASHVILLE • MELBOURNE • VANCOUVER

A Life Just Like Mine

How God and Nursing Turned Past Pain into Present Peace

Published in New York, New York, by Morgan James Publishing. Morgan James is a trademark of Morgan James, LLC. www.MorganJamesPublishing.com

Proudly distributed by Publishers Group West®

Scripture taken from the New King James Version® of the Bible. Copyright ©1982 by Thomas Nelson. Used by permission. All rights reserved.

Morgan James BOGO™

A **FREE** ebook edition is available for you or a friend with the purchase of this print book.

CLEARLY SIGN YOUR NAME ABOVE

Instructions to claim your free ebook edition:
1. Visit MorganJamesBOGO.com
2. Sign your name CLEARLY in the space above
3. Complete the form and submit a photo of this entire page
4. You or your friend can download the ebook to your preferred device

ISBN 9781636981604 paperback
ISBN 9781636981611 ebook
Library of Congress Control Number:
2023933177

Cover & Interior Design by:
Christopher Kirk
www.GFSstudio.com

Morgan James is a proud partner of Habitat for Humanity Peninsula and Greater Williamsburg. Partners in building since 2006.

Get involved today! Visit: www.morgan-james-publishing.com/giving-back

For all who chose to love me.

Contents

Acknowledgments

.

I am thankful for being accepted into the Morgan James family of writers. What a blessing to work with professionals with the mutual goal to provide hope through education and encouragement to inspire and provide life change. Thank you for believing in me.

I am grateful for those who give of their time and talents to equip Christian writers by presenting at conferences and workshops. Encouragement and support from these professionals provide needed stick-to-itiveness to complete a manuscript proposal and hit the submit button. Thank you, Terry Whalin, for your testimony, kindness, and encouragement every step of this process.

Knowing a person cannot be good at everything, I am most grateful for those who spend their life diving into manuscripts wielding an editing scalpel. Cutting and pasting with surgical precision, you clean up my messy grammar and punctuation. You have my heartfelt thanks and respect. Thanks to Larry Leech and Dr. Martha Friz-Langer for your editorial prowess. I will always be overwhelmed with gratitude for my helpful copy editor, Laura M. Bernhardt.

I am thankful for my diverse family of love and support. My Christian families: Sunshine Sisters, Walk to Emmaus, Blue Grass Church, nurse friends, Healthcare workers, and neighbors.

A special shout out to my sister, Patti Marie. I am so grateful for the phone calls and memories shared. This book would not be as accurate without you. Love you, Sissy.

I thank my one and only son, Will. I am so glad you are mine.

Thanks to my husband, Allen, who lets me follow any dream that strikes. Thank you for standing beside me. I don't ever want to walk through life without you.

Daily thanks to the God who chose to love me. Thank you for everything.

Chapter 1:

No Voice, No Choice

"**Y**oung lady, compose yourself," ordered the gruff, white-haired judge glaring down at me from his wooden perch. Perhaps wearing long, dark robes, pounding a desk with a wooden mallet, and years of standing in judgment of others removes all compassion from the heart. Then again, who has compassion to spare for a terrified twelve-year-old girl crying uncontrollably on the witness stand?

Compose yourself? This had to be some kind of legal terminology, for I had never heard that word before. Even if I had known the meaning, his demand was totally irrational. If this man with so much education, social status, and legal power had a brain in his head or a child of his own, he might have considered the view from the witness box. The title "Your Honor" should only be applied to humans with supernatural abilities: exceptional sensitivity, eagle eyes and keen hearing. Through broken-hearted sobs, I looked at that judge. Why couldn't he hear that screaming voice inside my head?

"This isn't right. This shouldn't be. This is so wrong."

Dad's attorney approached and began to bark out embarrassing questions. "On such and such a day, at such and such a time, you were seen by your brother in the living room of your home sitting on the couch beside a guy. He had his arm around you. Is this true? How old are you? Have you ever been kissed? How old was this man you were with?" His badgering ended with this accusatory implication: ". . . and where was your mother?"

Unbelievable. A first kiss, a first hug, on trial because I left some clothes at Dad's house? My mother and the boy's mother were having coffee in the kitchen, something friends often do. Did that really matter to anyone? It didn't seem like it should.

As if on cue, Dad jumped to his feet and shouted, "She's going to be a whore, just like her mother." Wildly waving his arms and pointing his finger at me, he screamed over and over again, "She's going to be a whore."

What a lovely prophecy to proclaim over me to a room full of people.

I never said a word, only sobbed. What else could I do? I was ushered out of the courtroom to the hallway to begin a lengthy course in the art of self-composure. Dumb and numb, like a lamb led to slaughter, I had no choice, no voice. I had no hand to hold, no shoulder to lean on, no one to dry my tears, and no one to pick up the pieces of a shattered heart.

Prior to the custody hearing, my parents had separated, not to anyone's surprise. I lived with Mom, which meant a steady diet of stewed anger towards Dad. Forced visitation with Dad meant hearing vivid, nasty stories about Mom. Dad didn't want me or my little sister. He simply didn't want Mom to have us. He wanted—and kept—my brother. At one point, Dad drove me through a trailer court and pointed out a blue-trimmed white trailer. A foster family lived there.

"Don't you think you would love it here? I can't afford to take care of you girls and these people can give you a great home. What do you think, honey?"

I didn't know what to think. It was like when I had jumped off the rope swing and slipped on the roots hiding under the leaf pile and broken my arm when I was five. I screamed, scared and hurting, my wrist dangling limp. I had no idea what had happened. I just knew something didn't feel right. People I don't know giving me a home? Dad's plan didn't feel right either.

On another visit, Dad broke a hundred-dollar bill to buy me something that cost five dollars and said, "Can't you see how much I love you now?" A five-dollar bill or a rusty trailer is not found in Webster's when you look up "love."

The outcome of the custody hearing gave my maternal grandparents custody, and that same night we left my favorite rental house forever. We threw our stuff into suitcases and tossed them into the trunk of the green Karmann Ghia. Then Mom and I made the trip over the rivers and through the woods to Grandmother's house.

Mom raked the gears and angrily cursed at the clutch. The car jerked violently uphill, stalling several times. There was no need for embarrassment. I would no longer live on this street.

During the two-hour trip, Mom explained the rationale behind her choice. "You have to understand one thing," she said. "No one is ever going to tell me what to do. No one judge has any right to tell me who I will see and who I won't. That judge gave me an ultimatum. I could keep you girls if I stop seeing Rip. You need to understand. You are going to live with your grandparents because no one is going to run my life. No one tells me what to do."

Rip. What an appropriate name for the one who tore my family to shreds! Memories can get lost over time, yet some sit in storage in the warehouse of our minds. They wait for us to rewind and review them in living color, with real emotion and exact dialog. Tragic life scenes can be a bit entertaining from a distance, like an angry redhead with a lead foot speeding around the crooked roads through the hills and valleys of Pennsylvania in the darkness, on her way to drop off her children, who have less value to her than her lover.

Why did she speed? Why did she drive all night? The next morning was the first day of Junior High. I faked sleep, leaning my weary head against the passenger window. My tear buckets were depleted, but my thoughts overflowed. Goodbye, life—ballet, tap, baton, friends, brother, dog. No time to say goodbye. Perhaps they'll miss me? Maybe no one will notice or care. They'll think I've died. I have.

Chapter 2:

Major Moves, Minor Memories

Moving means leaving things and people you love behind. Some you never see again. We moved four times in a two-year period, while I was in the sixth and seventh grades. Each move felt like we were searching for a home away from home.

The first move was the hardest for my siblings and me. Our home, for those first eleven years before the divorce, had been Daddy's pride and joy. White, red, and deep purple petunias lined the front walk of the white-painted concrete block ranch style home. It had three bedrooms, and featured an open floor plan with huge plate glass windows in the living room and dining room that filled our home with light on sunny days. Around the bar in the kitchen, we spent time doing homework while either Dad or Mom cooked.

Mature trees, perfect for climbing, surrounded the swing set. A neighborhood with gobs of kids of every age gave our childhood the best jumpstart for life. Oh, how we loved the outdoors. Woods nestled up to our back yard, and Dad had created a basketball court in a rear corner of the property. He had also purchased the neighboring field from Mrs. Winslow, the widow next door, where we played baseball, kickball, or badminton. Like Spanky and the Little Rascals, our life was full of friends, fun and adventure.

We lived close to the construction of Interstate 79 in Meadville, Pennsylvania. Smooth new roads, not yet open to traffic, became a new playground for our neighborhood clan. My brother Terry was two or three years older than I, and he was always full of fun and adventure. Even though my sister Patti was five years younger than I, she was fearless and eager to do anything the big kids did.

We rode our bikes for miles on the newly paved interstate. Sometimes Lady, our liver and white springer spaniel, came along to swim in the creek beneath the overpass. Once in the water, she paddled like an Olympian. Afterward, she would trudge up the embankment, shake like a wild thing, and run up to us long enough to get pats of love. Then she would jump back in the creek and do it all over again. She loved it, and we all loved her.

Supper always felt like an intrusion in our playing time. After we ate, we helped with dishes and then rushed back outside. We poked holes in jar lids and scrambled around the yard catching bugs with bulbs in their little butts, and voila! We had an electrified mason jar for free. When darkness fell, we armed ourselves with flashlights to enjoy another adventurous challenge. We would sweep the ground with our flashlights as if they were spotlights and, quick as a robin, pounce on any big, juicy nightcrawler we found for Daddy to go fishing. Those were the days BD—Before Divorce.

Dad and Mom worked separate shifts. Dad worked evenings at Talon Zipper factory and Mom worked nights at the Viscose plant. She slept during the day while we were in school and sometimes took another nap before her eleven o'clock shift.

Mom chauffeured us kids to dance, swimming, and guitar lessons during the week. Dad helped on the weekends. Saturday mornings, Patti and I marched up the steep staircase of the dance studio where we both hoped our dreams would come true. For as long as I could remember, all I had ever wanted to be was a dancer.

Our circle of friends grew as recitals and parades were added to our schedule. Mom sewed our costumes full of sequins and netting and worked with other mothers on how to construct headbands and tutus. Whatever shortcomings she might have had, Mom had a talent for sewing and knitting. If she had her hands on a pattern for anything, perfection reigned every time. Blessed with the ability to decipher the most difficult crochet, knitting or sewing patterns, Mom thrived on the challenge of creating something. Before our birthdays, she set up the sewing machine on the dining room table and the next morning, Barbie, Ken, Midge, and Skipper all had custom made wardrobes for every season. Mom was a whiz. We knew if Mom made anything, it would be a one-of-a-kind creation that would last forever. I guess that was why the divorce was so hard for us to understand.

Marriage doesn't come with a pattern, recipe, or guidebook. I wish it didn't come with challenges either, but it does. Mom was miserable and needed something more.

A solution came when she persuaded Dad to go dancing with several couples from her workplace. When Dad agreed, our home dynamic changed. Couples took turns going to each other's homes to whirl the blender full of crème de menthe and crème de cacao into some green concoction called a Grasshopper. They shared babysitters and grouped us kids at one home or another while drinking or dining out replaced our private family movie night. Before, we had loved spending Sunday nights sprawled out on the living room floor snuggled in blankets and pillows, eating popcorn Daddy made for us. Our Sunday night family tradition had meant tuning in to the Wonderful World of Disney. Now on Sundays a neighbor would come and babysit us. Family time somehow got lost. We kids looked hard but never did find it.

Fights between Mom and Dad became a common occurrence. Anger grew and criticism flew. Because she was obsessed with TV soap operas, Mom set her sleep schedule so that she would not miss Days of Our Lives. We could have stocked several libraries with copies of True Love magazines. When Dad was working, Mom could lie down on the floor or couch for hours, bawling to LPs of Eddie Arnold love songs and Ray Price singing "For the Good Times."

Like a record Mom had a flip side. Her A-side was fun, but her B-side was trouble. I think someone mentioned the term "rage-a-holic," and my brother and I knew its meaning all too well. Being on the receiving end of redheaded rage sometimes left claw marks down my back, but the soul scars hurt more. At least they were invisible, and no one ever saw the scary side of Mom but us.

I'll never forget the time Patti and Terry were playing ball in the living room, which was a big no-no. The ball accidentally struck Mom's favorite tall, orange-flecked pitcher, scattering glass fragments like dead soldiers all over the black and white linoleum tile floor. When Mom came through the front door with an armload of groceries, I somehow ended up on the martyr chopping block. Terry announced convincingly, "Donna did it."

Ignoring my pleas of innocence, Mom jerked my arm, threw down the groceries, pushed and pulled me into the kitchen and whipped away at me. She bared her teeth, thrusting out her lower jaw with a wild-eyed evil glare, and words saturated with swearing accompanied the beating. My siblings confessed long after the whipping ceased, but no one can take back a beating. No one can erase that moment or memory.

Change kept happening as new terms and phrases became a part of our life: separation, custody, hearings, child support, and infidelity. We learned that a trial separation period meant Dad had to go. He moved out to a tiny apartment with only a hot plate upon which to cook. During his weekend visitation, he took us to church. At the end of the service, we would all troop down to the altar to pray. Daddy begged God to heal his marriage and save his family. I never saw him so ripped up. Faith in God was always important to my dad. He taught the adult Sunday School class, sang special music with his smooth tenor voice, and loved to read his Bible.

One night while Mom and we three kids were still living in our house, my uncle came to convince her not to leave Dad. They were up all night fighting and crying. Words were muffled. Strange phrases that I didn't understand hit my ears. He kept saying, "Stay for the kids. If I can, so can you." He couldn't convince her.

During all this fighting, uncertainty, and change, something happened to me. I got sick. Doctors put me in a private isolation room in the hospital to be sure that whatever I had wasn't contagious. No one knew what was wrong for days. They prodded me with slick gloves in private places with no warning, stuck needles in my arms and sucked out blood like Barnabas Collins in Dark Shadows (my brother and I used to run home from the bus stop every afternoon to watch that vampire show together).

People couldn't come to visit me without putting on disposable plastic gowns and gloves. My food was served on disposable paper plates using plastic silverware. I felt like a leper. No one touched me. I felt like whatever was wrong could kill me and all those around me.

I was scared and, like always, I wasn't hungry. For years the neighborhood kids nicknamed me after a skinny fashion model, Twiggy. I didn't like to eat. Mom often yelled at me, "There are starving kids in Biafra." I would say, "Get their addresses and we can mail them my food."

Daddy went to great lengths to cheer me up. About a week into my hospital stay, he and Terry brought Lady to the hospital parking lot. I called out to her from my fourth-floor hospital window. She jumped up and down and turned in circles trying to find me. She pulled frantically on the leash, whimpering and confused. I wished I could have flown out my window. I needed to bury my face in her fluffy, soft curls, rub her belly and brush her. She remained out of my reach. I watched the station wagon pull away and knew no matter what, I had to get well and go home.

Delores, one of Mom's closest friends, stepped up to the plate after I was discharged with the embarrassing diagnosis of malnutrition. A marvelous cook, she offered to help me get stronger in a stress-free, more stable environment. Recuperation with Delores, her husband Rip, and her daughter Diann seemed a good idea at first.

Diann was an only child who loved her dad and the family's black and white bulldogs. She also could down two liters of soda like crazy. We became quick friends, rode motor bikes, slept together every night and shared secrets. Best of all, we walked to church every Sunday. None of the adults in this new living situation ever went to church, so it was just us two girls.

During this time, Daddy, Terry, and Patti Marie still lived at home, until one afternoon Mom and Delores kidnapped Patti when she got off the bus. Helpless, Dad stood in the driveway with a dishcloth over his shoulder, and watched the two women push Patti into the car. Totally ignoring the little girl's cries for her dad, they took off.

About one week after my hospitalization, what I thought to be a temporary situation turned into the first of many moves. An attic bedroom was made for Mom and Patti. A brown thing hung from the ceiling. Rip had been a boxer and explained it was a speed bag. Tying mitts on us, he tried to teach us how to use it. He kept up an exercise and weightlifting routine daily, along with smoking several packs of cigarettes. He always prided himself on never drinking a beer before three o'clock. After three, however, those empty cans piled up.

Lady even lived with us for a little while, in a cage in the garage with Rip's four Brittany spaniels. She couldn't live in the house because bulldogs took precedence over spaniels.

During the month we lived with Rip and Delores, Diann was diagnosed with juvenile diabetes, what we now call type 1 diabetes. She had to take insulin shots and eat differently. Her mom took to the diet, medication, and care regimen with gusto. Diann fell apart. I felt so sorry for her. She tested her urine with a dip stick several times a day and had to be careful with food. When you are a teenager, it's hard to accept a physical problem connected with a bunch of complications that can ruin your health.

Diabetes happens, you don't choose it. Divorce happens, and kids usually don't choose that either. I know Diann and I wouldn't have chosen these life-changing memories of loss. When a marriage train derails, all passengers experience the jolt. Diann and I did.

As we were lying in the sun, lathered in oil and laughing and talking one Sunday afternoon, we overheard something children could never want to hear. The word "divorce" got our attention. Rip, Delores, and Mom were fighting and yelling obscenities at each other. Rip got in Delores's face and laid out his case. "I don't love you anymore. I love her. I want a divorce and that's final. There's nothing more to say. Our marriage is over." We watched the whole backyard scene; it was like a soap opera with nasty language.

Wow! Dad's stories might have been true after all. Mom and Rip had a thing going on, like the song, "Me and Mrs. Jones" by Billy Paul. Without a doubt, another move was imminent. So was another loss. I never saw Delores, Diann, or Lady again.

Our second move away from home was a quick fix getaway in the form of a trailer. Patti and I didn't have many of our toys or clothes, because they were still at our old home. For kids who loved to be outside, it was hard to be surrounded by concrete, few trees, and no lightning bugs or nightcrawlers. But Mom seemed content and loved to say, "There's a place for everything and everything is in its place."

My role changed from big sister to an armed guard. If Dad stopped by to see us and bring us candy, I'd grab Patti, push her inside, and lock the door. Then we talked through the screen. Patti cried, "He's my daddy." Afraid of the wrath of Mom, I became an enemy in the eyes of my sister, a true no-win situation for me.

After we spent six months living with the stigma of being called trailer trash, a rental house on Oak Street became available. Move number three was the best move of all. That house held great memories for me. It had been the home of one of my best friends from dance class, Jill. I can't count how many times I spent the night there. I loved her mom; she was good to us.

Jill and I had a great deal in common. We loved dance and, like me, her parents were going through a nasty divorce. Jill was a tall, long haired, redhead and a crazy-good acrobat. I think instead of joints, God gave her springs.

She and her mother moved to a townhouse while her dad created an upstairs efficiency apartment with a separate entranceway. He then rented the downstairs to Mom, Patti, and me. We actually stayed put for an entire year.

I made friends, rode the bus to school, and even got my first babysitting job for a family with three kids up the street. Our rental house had a front and back yard with mature trees. I loved to read on the porch off the bedroom. Finally, I felt we had settled in. Patti and I spent lots of time together. One major joy for me was when Mom allowed me to walk back and forth to dance class alone. During Crawford County Fair preparation, I must have walked miles, for we practiced several times a day in the summer. I never minded. I was happy.

Dad and Terry still lived at home, but my memories aren't clear. I don't remember going there often. I did miss Lady. She was still at Rip's house.

Mom might have known that, because she surprised Patti and me with puppies: Honeybee and Mitzie Lee, two miniature black and white bulldogs. Rip loved to play with them when he came to see Mom. Since he and Mom worked nights together at the plant, he stopped by for coffee in the mornings before we got on the school bus.

As the custody hearing date moved up on the calendar, strange parental behaviors showed up too. Daddy appeared shamelessly and frequently on the neighbor's porch directly across the street and sat in a lawn chair, watching us through binoculars. Mom told us to ignore him, not to wave or make a fuss. It seemed so odd for Dad to be on a stranger's porch. I wondered what he told those people. I wondered what they thought of my mom and Patti and me. When someone peers at you like a "Peeping Tom", it is embarrassing. I think it's more embarrassing when "Tom" is spelled D-A-D.

After our day in court, my fourth and furthest move meant leaving more than ever behind: so many people and things I would never see again, so many people I never even had the opportunity to tell "Goodbye, I'm leaving; here's my address; please write me." Never again would I dress in my black leotard and pink tights and wear my satin pointe shoes or tap shoes. Never again would I dance.

Once, while I was visiting my grandparents when I was nine, their dog, Betsy, had chewed up and ruined my favorite book, To Dance, To Dream. I tried to salvage my book, but I had to throw it away. As hard as it is, sometimes dreams have to go, too.

Chapter 3:

Another Place, Another Time

M ove number four landed Patti and me on a five-acre plot in the country. Truth bit me hard. My sister and I would be on our own, alone, without Mom or Dad. The scary part was we didn't know Mom's parents, and they did not know us. Like a foster family, we were simply strangers stuck together in a cramped little house.

Spending time with grandparents during the holidays is not the same as sharing a living space. Learning routines, house rules, responsibilities and expectations takes time. After living in different households, Patti and I had learned to go with the flow with few objections. No matter where we lived, Mom had laid down all the rules and we followed every one of them. But now, she gladly handed all responsibility, decision-making, and correction over to her parents.

Once again, we faced the unknown. Patti and I had to start a new life on a strange bus filled with kids we didn't know and jump off at a new school with new rules, while Mom happily drove two hours home to Rip and freedom.

On our first day of school, Grandpa pounded on our wooden bedroom door, opened it, snapped on the blinding overhead light, and announced, "Girls get up; you have to catch the bus. Come and eat breakfast. Hurry up. Don't dillydally." Resurrection by ceiling light and verbal thunder was a totally different alarm system that became routine. I grew to hate the daily rude awakening.

Another thing I missed was a good night's sleep. We got up early since we now lived over an hour away from school. There's nothing like waiting for the school bus in the dark, but I'm sure the yellow flashing lights helped the driver see us and stop.

Nudging Patti, I crawled out of bed, smoothed the log cabin quilt and rushed to the bathroom. Oh, it was so small and so strange. The left side of the bathroom was all appliance: white porcelain tub, sink, and toilet. All of the sinks I had used before possessed a single faucet, but in this sink, there were two. They took sides on the basin, and like some marriages they stood separate, running purely cold or hot.

As I glanced up at my own horrific image in the rust-speckled medicine cabinet mirror, I wondered how eyelids could be so puffy. Who on earth had drawn dark half-moons under my eyes? Only vampires flaunt blood red eyes. I hoped the kids didn't think I was a vampire. "Tattletale" is a perfect name for eyes and faces. No one can hide sadness, sleeplessness, loneliness, and the fear of being unacceptable and friendless. If only warm water and Ivory soap could magically transform my weary face…Enough.

Gently shaking Patti's shoulders, I said, "Sleepyhead, get up. We have to eat and get to school."

"Okay, I'm up already." Sifting through the suitcase on the floor, she picked out a favorite outfit and headed for the bathroom. I asked, "Do you know what day this is?"

Turning up her nose, she scowled. "I'm not stupid. It's the first day of school."

"Well, it happens to be September 8, 1970, which means you are eight years old, and this is your birthday. Happy Birthday, little sister."

"Well, if this is my birthday, all I want is to go home. I don't want to live here. I don't want to go to a new school. I want to go home."

Patti Marie always knew exactly what she wanted and never held emotions in check. Her brown hair curled like a living Shirley Temple doll—a very spoiled, spicy, sassy doll whose mischievous smile opened the door marked, "Cutie, whatever you want you get." Today's behavior was totally normal. She stomped down the hall, and I wished I could make that birthday wish happen somehow for both of us.

Using the antique mirror in the bedroom, I slapped on makeup and wondered what else had taken place yesterday in the courtroom. Bad behavior from both parties obliterated character witness testimonies. Mom had told me the judge made a different kind of plea. "Is there anyone here who would take these two girls and raise them?"

My maternal grandparents, the Cowans, accepted the challenge, with Dad required to pay twenty-five dollars per month in child support. At first, the rules and regulations handed down by the judge seemed harsh. We soon found out Grandma's rules were even more severe, with consequences that scorched everyone.

Gram bossed Grandpa unashamedly, and if a college of manipulation existed, she would have graduated with multiple honors. Our dysfunctional family dynamic provided Gram with a new obsession—controlling Rip.

If Rip came with Mom for visitation, Gram would shake her right pointer finger one-fourth of an inch from his nose, deftly stiffen it like the beak of a pileated woodpecker, and tap on his breast bone fifty times while singing the same old song to the tune of righteousness. "Don't think for a minute you will be sleeping together in my house. You're living in sin. Why buy a cow when you can get the milk for free? If she's good enough to sleep with, she's good enough to marry." If he heard that once, he heard it a thousand times. We all did.

Other restrictions included absolutely no alcohol, smoking or bad language in Gram's house. Drinking and smoking was always a no-no, even for my uncle. When he came to visit, which was not often, cold beer lay ready in the cooler of the Suburban. He drank and smoked in the driveway.

Rip loved cigarettes, beer, and creative renditions of cuss words. I never understood why a person would want to corrupt an innocent, meaningful word like "fantastic" by pulling apart its syllables and folding in a nasty four-letter word.

Cuss words seemed to be essential supports for conversation between Mom and Dad. I always cut Dad slack because he had served in World War II. Mom kind of followed Rip's lead and nasty language tagged along. Even now, all these years later, I cringe when I think of the words they used.

Dad and Mom could never visit at the same time, which created stress during holidays. Before the divorce, we kids had always loved the anticipation of gifts, good food and time together. Those days were gone. An actual holiday date lost all meaning. A new disappointment arrived, and I named the newbie, "holiday stretch out." Holiday celebrations happened when our parents weren't working, and instead of one holiday we had to have three. Sometimes the stretch was over a week or two, which seemed to be an abnormal way to celebrate. Christmas left us empty every year.

Mom loved Christmas, and we had always put up a huge tree in the living room decorated with lights, balls, teardrops, and tinsel. At Gram's a table-top imposter replaced a cherished real tree from the woods. Sustaining a fresh cut tree for multiple visitations required too much work. Gram reiterated repeatedly how needles turn brown and fall, the limbs bow down, and the tree dries and dies. My response: "But Gram, the smell of a real tree in the house makes Christmas." Sharing my feelings never moved her an inch. I began to dread holidays and despise happy memories.

At the old house, when we had lived together as a family, we always sang carols and danced to Christmas music. We slathered scissors with butter and cut mint, cinnamon, and wild flavors of hard tack candy into pieces and flopped them into bags of powdered sugar. We made the best chocolate fudge ever with chunks of walnuts. Mom made divinity candy to die for and cookie press cookies with red hots and silver balls. My favorite cookies were gingersnaps and Russian tea cakes, which we all sampled hot from the oven with a big glass of cold milk. Mom stuffed dates with icing and made peanut brittle that melted in your mouth. We packed tins with our confections and gifted them to teachers, neighbors, and friends in the old neighborhood. Once upon a time, I loved Christmas.

Now we lived in another time.

Chapter 4:

Life's Pantry

The saying, "You don't know what you've got until it's gone" became reality for Patti and me, and maybe even for our grandparents. I doubt couples in their sixties scribble "raising our daughter's two girls" on their dream list of things to do before retirement. Weeding, planting, snapping, peeling, freezing, preparing food, and doing dishes (so many dishes…) doesn't make it to the top ten of kids' lists either.

If work and play were kids on a teeter-totter, balance could never happen at Gram's house. Work outweighed play daily for Patti and me, but I believe sacrifices of displacement create a life imbalance for everyone.

Grandpa worked as a mechanic at the Ford garage. He got up before the sun, ate breakfast, grabbed his sturdy silver lunch box, and drove forty-five minutes to and from work. He was never late, and he was never sick. Gram gave up her job cooking and baking at the county home to don a stay-at-home Super-Grandma cape.

Priorities changed. Patti Marie and I found ourselves in the awkward presence of people obsessed with food. Our grandparents' need to stockpile, prepare, and share food probably resulted from growing up during the depression. The downstairs cabinet pantry shelves Grandpa built held pints and quarts of canned vegetables and fruits of every kind. Every Friday night our family went to town, and like people stocking a restaurant, we bought food—lots of it.

Our first stop was always the grocery store. There was no such thing as buying one can of fruit or a couple cans of pumpkin. If it was on sale, Grandpa bought cases. As we traveled down country roads to the meat house, I watched the black Angus cattle milling about on the hillside. I wondered if the farmer's kids named the cows. If so, who would we be eating next month?

Our next stop required speeding down narrow dirt or gravel roads to an old farmhouse out in nowhere-land to get churned butter and eggs. What a different way to spend a Friday night! We got back home after dark, unpacked the car, packaged the meats, and filled the freezers.

We lived on five acres. Each spring we designed about three acres with vegetables, fruits, and flower gardens. Gram loved dahlias. Imagine perfect, vibrant flowers of striking colors wearing shades of purple, orange, yellow, pink, red, and white, imitating three-inch pompoms or layers of stars the size of dinner plates. These tender perennials were stored in heavy milk crates under the house in the winter to protect them from the severe cold. In the spring, because I was small, I had the pleasure of jumping through the rectangular foundation hole to grab and hand out the sleeping beauties. Just like people, dahlia tubers need support as they grow, so we would dig a hole and bury a stake beside the tuber, so when storms rain down, stalks wouldn't break and heads wouldn't "hang down, Tom Dooley."

Several varieties of plum and apple trees bloomed on my grandparents' property, giving Grandpa pitching pleasure. He loved to throw a piece of ripe fruit to anyone at any time. In the fall, I pretended to be the queen of the fallen apple. I would climb and gently shake the apple tree limbs as I imagined apples singing, "Please release me let me go." Once on the ground, I transformed into a servant child, picking up the fallen fruit. Once my basket was filled, I headed to the kitchen to wash, core, and skin the apples. It was lots of work for lots of lasting pleasure. Nothing comes close to fresh apple pie, homemade apple sauce, or apple butter on a cold winter evening.

Laundry became an all-day affair in the musty basement. We began the day by positioning the big white monster of a wringer washer tub near the drain in the basement floor, plugging it into the electrical outlet in the ceiling turning on its red garden-like hoses of hot and cold water, adding detergent, and cautiously taking position. Multiple trips down the basement steps with armloads of clothes, sheets, quilts, rugs, and rags, stole the day away. Color-sorted piles on the gray concrete floor patiently waited to be grabbed up, baptized, and agitated. We would wash, rinse, squeeze and toss things into clothes baskets and once again do step aerobics, running up the storm cellar steps to the clothesline outside.

Wringer washer orientation included tragic stories of deformed arms, hands or boobs getting caught in rollers. Gram was at risk for the latter; she had a forty-four-inch bust that Grandpa proudly adored, as he called her his "little Dolly Parton."

This weekly laundry process gave clothes a smell no softener has ever captured. Sunshine and "fersh" air (Gram's pronunciation). Snow and ice never halted cleanliness, and I gained the art of folding freeze-dried sheets and underclothes. It was quite a crunchy, finger-numbing experience hanging clothes up wet and taking them down stiff.

One Christmas, Grandpa bought an electric washer and a dryer, hooked it up in the basement, put a great big red bow on the dryer, and told Gram she never needed another Christmas gift. Every year, that red bow appeared on the dryer as a reminder of the gift that keeps on giving.

Every week, people showed up to Gram's tiny kitchen to enjoy homemade feasts of rolls, cookies, pies, or a huge meal. Curiosity grabbed me and I asked one day, "Gram, why do we work so hard to can, freeze and stockpile food, then cook like dogs and feed people all the time?"

"That's just what we do," she told me.

When a person does something extremely well, people give praise. Gram cooked like a renowned country chef. She loved to feed people. More than anything, she loved the praise. She had a habit of politely asking, "Would you like another helping?" If the person declined, she filled a spoon of veggies, meat, or potatoes, slapped it on the person's plate and said, "Of course, you do." We called it "force feeding."

Patti Marie and I often wished we used paper plates more often to lighten our workload. Gram christened us with the daily chore of washing and drying dishes at suppertime and when company came.

After feeding the crowd, we cleared the dining room table, which was really in the living room. We then pushed the table up against the wall and window to make room for people to sit on the couches and chairs. We felt like fish in a fishbowl, as privacy evaded us while we scrubbed every dish, pot and pan and then put away leftovers. Patti and I couldn't talk without listening ears.

When the kitchen was spotless, our next duty was like sitting in a prison. If we wanted to go out to play, go to our bedroom to read a book, or if it was a school night and we wanted to go to bed, Gram denied our wishes. She forced us to sit quietly in the living room listening to the grownups' chatter. If we begged to go to bed, Gram's evil eye screamed as she faked a meek smile and sweetly said, "Girls, we've got company."

One evening, Bill and Thelma, neighbors from down the road, came for supper and Gram dished out the gravy, meat, and vegetables. My job was to carry everything to the table down the open passageway from the kitchen to the living room. The last dish was Gram's famous hand-whipped mashed potatoes dotted with "cow-butter" (Patti's name for the deep yellow rounds of churned butter she refused to eat once she knew it came from cows. We never told her about milk). Gram handed me the heavy mountain of spuds sprinkled with pepper and perfectly positioned parsley sprigs, heaped three inches higher than the china bowl. "Now, whatever you do," she warned me, "don't you dare drop this."

Whoosh! The bowl crashed to the floor. Potatoes, butter, pepper and parsley redecorated everything within spattering distance. Mashed taters flew into the living room, spreading smooth spuds in a six-inch landing strip on Gram's beloved olive-green wall-to-wall carpet.

Devastated, I tried to explain. "Oh no, I swear the bowl never touched my hands."

Gram's evil eye, clutched jaw and visage of total disgust transformed the hostess into a four-foot, eleven-inch angry demon while I scurried to clean up the mess. Everyone at the table saw Gram reaching into the cabinet above the stove for a box of Hungry Jack instant potatoes to save the day. The hostess never returned to the table, but the demon did. I tried hard to regain composure as I sobbed and sniffed in shame, head down to avoid Gram's glare.

A strange sound caused me to glance at Bill. He was trying hard to stifle snorts and laughter while he watched Gram shoot me with an eye-gun loaded with bullets of disgust. Chuckling, he announced, "Kiddo, if dropping a bowl of mashed potatoes is the worst thing you ever do in life, I think you're gonna make it."

Gram smirked, smiled, then laughed, and everyone relaxed and joined in.

I wondered if Gram was mad that I dropped the potatoes or embarrassed that the neighbors knew Hungry Jack lived in our cabinet. Some memories carry, strengthen, and help a wounded, embarrassed klutz. Circumstances often allow us opportunities to share these meaningful life lessons. A healthy perspective and laughter can serve people well when they make a big mess.

Chapter 5:

How Do You Define Family?

The need to belong and be loved by others is universal. Family dynamics could easily meet that need. Thanks to my dad, a broader definition of family resulted from a stipulation in the divorce decree. Church attendance was an expectation, not an option, and it created an exceptional extended family full of creativity, personalities, and talents.

In order to avoid violating the decree and getting a whipping from Dad's attorney, Grandpa made sure we took our places on the hard-wooden pews at the non-denominational Christian church on the hill less than half a mile from the house. Any time the church doors were open, we were there. I doubt the congregation knew the Cowan family Sunday rituals.

We got up before dawn, donned our work clothes, and gathered in the kitchen. Iron skillets hit the gas stove, bacon and eggs sizzling in one, pork chops browning in another. Gram sliced homemade bread for toast while one of us washed, peeled, and sliced potatoes paper thin and tossed them into the speckled roaster for scalloped potatoes and chops. Breakfast and lunch were ready in less than twenty minutes. We ate quickly and then headed for the garden.

Snipping greenery, lilacs, delphinium and dahlias from rows and rows of blooms, Gram created the arrangements for the front of the church every Sunday. Once the arrangements were perfected, we jumped into the car. Grandpa sped us up to the church to position milk glass vases full of flowers on the wooden stands on each side of pastor's podium.

We scrambled back home, cleaned the kitchen, and set the table for lunch. All four of us needed to wash up, change clothes and get to church on time (or, if Grandpa got his way, early). If Patti and I ran late, Grandpa and Gram sat in the car while he laid on the horn. As if that made us faster!

After church people always came to eat with us. Some were friends, some were strangers, but all were willing to enjoy a Dottie Cowan feast. The Lord rested on Sunday. Patti and I labored. Little did we know Gram's expert training from those days made us great cooks. I doubt Dad knew that either.

Gram and Grandpa despised Dad. Yet even hot anger can pop out goodness like popcorn. Add heat to a moisture-filled corn kernel, and in a short time expansion and a tiny explosion creates a crunchy culinary delight. Because of steamy, simmering distrust, Grandpa never spent one cent of Dad's child support; he was convinced somehow that payback lurked in the future. Just the same, unexpected goodness popped. Grandpa learned to save money.

Exposure to church opened a new door of entertainment for our family. Grandpa had always loved music. He collected albums of country and western singers and polkas, and we watched *The Lawrence Welk Show* and *Hee Haw* every week. We became gospel quartet groupies, traveling to tiny neighboring villages and churches to hear them sing. We traveled for hours to hear fantastic evangelical preachers preach sermons ripe with rapture, while harmonies of gospel groups gave us soundbites from heaven.

Surprising everyone, Grandpa joined the men's choir at church. Nerve deafness left him tone deaf, but because his character gave him perfect pitch, no one minded or ever said a thing. He stood proud and tall every Sunday in the back row of the choir loft, smiling as he sang his heart out with his newfound friends and neighbors. He truly made a joyful noise. One night, he asked Gram how to become a Christian, and she led him in the sinner's prayer. He truly meant it when he sang, "I'm so glad I'm a part of the family of God."

Faith lessons learned didn't only come from the pastor, but also from the lives of God-loving women, fifty-plus years older than me. I began to see God through Verna, Ethel, Valley, Mary, and Enie.

Verna was the church pianist, and like Grandpa, she also suffered hearing loss. This frequently caused controlled chaos during Sunday service. In a booming voice, Pastor Bob would shout out the hymn numbers that were posted on the wall beyond Verna's view. Bulletins did not exist, so there was no other way to know what the hymns would be for the service. Strange chords of dissonance rang as he started singing the first few words of his selection. We knew Verna was playing something entirely different. Let the flip and find game begin! If Pastor announced that the hymn was on page 356, we quickly scanned our hymnals with the speed of NASCAR drivers nearing the last lap. Was Verna playing the hymn from page three, page fifty, page fifty-six, or page six? Whoever found the page would message everyone else the number with their fingers, and we joined dear, oblivious Verna in the chorus or verse.

Verna truly marched to a different drummer. She was old, lean, and fragile, and she lived alone with no neighbors for miles. Refusing retirement, she worked once a week cleaning an attorney's office in the nearby town. She loved the Lord, and once told me why she never used a mop. "I clean and scrub down on my knees, so I can pray for the attorneys, office workers and all the people they help. I love to be so close to God."

One day a stranger came to Verna's door and asked to use her phone. She let him in without hesitation. He beat and raped her. The battered seventy-year-old woman came to church with a black, blue and purple face, a bruised jaw and a swollen left eye. Her hair was perfect as always, tucked in a bun under a little cream hat sporting a sprig of pastel pansies. She sat tall at the piano with a genuine smile and tickled the ivories as if nothing had happened. The drunk attacker was found and put in jail.

Instead of crying "Why me, God?" her love grew stronger than ever. She was thankful to be alive. The amazed congregation witnessed faith on fire, courage supplied by grace, saintly praise and resolute resilience. It was a terrible, personal, physically abusive trauma, and Verna moved on.

Ethel lived back down the Sharp Road, a single lane dirt road sandwiched between thick woods on each side. She frequently popped into Gram's for tea, coffee and a piece of apple pie or whatever dessert sat on the counter. Once, as I waved goodbye to her from the porch while she was leaving the front driveway, she gave me a good scare. Ethel was looking back at me over her right shoulder as the car ambled forward, heading straight for Gram's beloved allspice bush and apple orchard.

I shouted in a panic, "Ethel, Ethel, stop! Stop!" Laughing, she stopped, put the car in reverse, shrugged and drove home. Is it any wonder I panicked?

When I told Grandpa what happened, he told me her backstory. In the early 1940s, Grandpa had owned and operated a garage twenty feet from the house. One day he spied Ethel's husband Meryl driving past and pulling into the driveway at the house. Slipping a mechanic's wrench into his coat pocket, Grandpa walked to the house in record time to see what Meryl was up to. Everyone knew Meryl loved alcohol more than anything, including Ethel.

"What's the problem, Meryl?"

"I need Dot. Ethel's sick. I need Dot to come with me and take care of her."

"No Meryl, Dot cannot leave our two babies She can call Doc Schaefer, and I'll come with you and help Ethel."

Drunken Meryl had forced Ethel to drink a bottle of Lestoil cleaner at gunpoint. Doc Schaefer pumped her stomach in the kitchen of their old farmhouse. The judge sentenced Meryl to one year of church attendance, which he completed, and then he never darkened a church door again. He died young. Ethel lived much, much longer.

When huge snowstorms hit and buried her driveway and road, friends and neighbors with snowmobiles flew over the drifts to deliver groceries and make sure Ethel was safe. She managed quite well for an emotionally and physically abused widow. When trouble arose, she often called Grandpa for help.

One spring day, she called Gram. "Dot, can you please send Mervin by quickly? I got too close to a tree with a low hanging limb while mowing. I just went limp, and it caught me at my waist and lifted me off the riding mower. Tell him to please come fetch my mower; it's headed for the north field. If he can't come, I guess it will eventually stop when it runs out of gas."

Another character in my life was Valley. She'd never had children, loved her sweet husband, and had to be one of the greatest joys of my life. One day when I was sixteen, she took me driving in her huge Cadillac.

"Now Donna," she said, "I just want you to know your granddad loves you very much and he prefers you drive thirty-five miles per hour for the rest of your days. However, you are a woman and sometimes we need to give it the gas. Here's the plan. We're going onto the interstate, and you just have to trust me." On the way up the ramp to I-80 towards Pittsburgh, Valley shouted, "Go girl, go! Let's move this baby! Pedal to the metal!"

Never in my life had I known anyone so full of verse as Valley. She had a poem for every thought, problem, or solution for life. She presented them with the flare of Auntie Mame. She recited every word and stanza from "If" by Rudyard Kipling. Valley gifted me with a poem of truth that became my forever favorite.

Some couples never can be parents, yet by sharing and caring for those like me, I learned a secret: "Motherhood" is a title. *Mothering* is a gift, an art, and a blessing shared by unselfish, loving women. Valley longed for and never had the privilege of childbirth. She never needed that experience to mother me or other young kids. When we realize the huge number of people in our lives who freely gift their love to us, gratefulness rises, emptiness falls, and unrealistic expectations of those who are unable to care for us in the way we need them to begin to fade.

Mary, the head of the school cafeteria, and Enie, a fantastic cafeteria helper, were friends who Gram knew and loved. They became my friends, too. School lunches were fit for royalty. They served mouth-watering homemade soups, meats, potatoes, country veggies, and desserts, but best of all were the huge yeast cinnamon rolls. The smell of yeast wafted down the school hallways, making it difficult to listen to our teachers over the sound of our growling stomachs. Enie and Mary fed us well.

The greatest thing about Enie was that she lived close to the school and worked Monday through Friday. If I needed to stay after school for any event, especially during winter, she let me stay with her. We slept together under heavy wool blankets in her cold, drafty two-story house.

One such night she cried. Her heartache? Call it "Jennifer syndrome": a mid-life crisis in the form of a younger woman had jumped on her husband. After years of marriage, he left Enie for someone else and broke her heart. "I just don't understand this," Enie said. "I can't imagine what the young girl sees in him."

"Oh, Enie, I am so sorry." Patting her bony, curved back, I said, "Divorce is hard and hurtful, that I know." Divorce is no respecter of persons, shows no partiality and can touch the life of some of the dearest people. My older friend, Enie, like a sister, taught me many truths. Divorce causes pain and can sour any life, but Enie refused to be bitter.

I want to be like Enie.

Chapter 6:

Contagious Changes

C hange happens. Whether we choose acceptance or resistance is influenced by tag-a-long companions like familiarity, maturity, and a friend named Time. After living together for four years, our foursome—Gram, Grandpa, Patti, and I— befriended change. We became a family unit, imperfect but more accepting of each other.

We hugged and kissed Gram and Grandpa good night and told them we loved them. Oddly, Grandpa started kissing Gram goodbye every morning on his way to work. Even Gram's glare dimmed and disappeared.

Harmony reigned when the tiny kitchen turned into our practice studio during meal preparation. Gram's rich alto blended well with my soprano as we sang of Jesus's love, the wonder of God, and "The Last Mile of the Way." We sounded good together, and I convinced Gram to sing a special with me at church.

While she had always been more comfortable working behind the scenes, preparing food or flower arranging, Gram now shared another gift with our church family. Sunday came. Arm in arm, Gram and I walked to the front of the church and stood behind the wooden pulpit to let our harmony ring. When the music stopped, a chorus of "amen" echoed on. Gram smiled, head nodding to the congregation as we made our way back to our pew. She gently and quickly squeezed my hand about twenty times. Those squeezes, a hallmark of holding Gram's hand, felt like love.

Sunday church and Bible study on Wednesday nights changed our life priorities. Reading the Bible rose to the top of Gram's daily activities. In the bathroom, across from the toilet, on the first step to the attic, a little white Bible lay open, ready for pages to turn. I confess, I even picked it up, marked Gram's spot with a piece of toilet paper, and enjoyed reading the red words Jesus spoke. Most believers would not consider a quiet time in a tiny bathroom, but it worked. It was the one private place in the house with a guarantee of no distraction.

Change requires risks. My decision to ask Grandpa for things I wanted without a Gram filter was frightening. Like everyone else, Grandpa always took cues from Gram, and honestly, the first few years, Patti Marie and I feared him. When we did something wrong, Gram threatened us, "Just wait until Mervin gets home." Nervous, we worried all evening wondering if she'd tattle on us. Grandpa had a temper, and we knew it.

If I wanted to spend the night with a friend, Gram asked Grandpa for me. Depending on how she framed the question, he knew exactly how she wanted him to answer. In a sugary sweet voice, she would say, "Merv, Donna wants to spend the night with a friend. She helped me clean all week." That's a "yes." If she didn't want me to go, a disgusted tone showed up. "Donna has been gone three nights this week and now she wants to spend the night with her girlfriend."

I had never asked Grandpa for anything without Gram clearance, but at fifteen, I changed. Courage showed up. One night in July, after supper, I asked, "Grandpa, can I try out for cheerleading? That means a lot of driving me back and forth to the games until I turn sixteen and get my driver's license. What do you think?"

"First of all," Grandpa sighed, leaning forward, both elbows on the arms of the captain's chair. He shook his head "no," and said "Don't get your hopes up. You're a country girl competing against city girls. City folk will always get what they go after and will choose each other. You don't have a chance."

"Well, if I did make cheerleading, you realize that's a lot of trips every week after school and on the weekends because we cheer at all wrestling matches, basketball, and football games. You really don't mind if I try out?" I tried hard not to get too excited. I avoided looking in Gram's direction and bit my lip to keep from smiling too much.

"Sure, you can try out, but I'm warning you, you don't have a chance."

After school, I practiced with the cheer squad, learned the pompom routines, and worked on flips, back walkovers, cartwheels, and splits. Judges picked a total of ten cheerleaders for football season. During basketball and wrestling we divided into squads of five when games and matches fell on the same nights.

The afternoon after final tryouts I called Grandpa from the payphone in the school hallway. "Grandpa," I sniffed and sighed, sniffed and sighed, "you were right I didn't make it."

"I told you, you wouldn't," he said. "I told you not to get your hopes up so stop bawling about it."

"Ha ha!" I yelled. "Gotcha! I'm teasing you Grandpa. I made it! I'm a cheerleader!"

His response was priceless. "You what? You, a cheerleader? Well, I'll be."

Of all my accomplishments during the five years of living with my grandparents, my success in becoming a cheerleader changed Grandpa. A lasting pride gleamed from his face when he sat on the bleachers enjoying the games. A myth dissolved. A country girl with no chance took a chance and was chosen, and she was not just anyone's girl. She was Mervin's granddaughter.

During breaks, I squeezed between cheering fans and sat with him. Prior to football season, a woman from town who appeared to have a lot of clout had wanted baton twirlers at the football games. She learned I twirled baton and offered to teach me and another student to twirl fire. Then there would be cheerleaders during the first and second halves of football games and one or two fire-baton twirlers during halftime. It was a bit much, but I loved it.

In gym class one day, I dismounted off the balance beam with a cartwheel, and my ulna snapped like a green bean. What good is a handicapped cheerleader with a broken forearm? I thought my cheering days were over, but they let me stay on the squad. I attended every game and match. Friends teased they could never do without my big mouth. When my cast came off, my arm was withered and weak. For the next tryouts, I taught myself one-handed cartwheels, back walkovers, and flips.

Determination and risk are a pair of characters worth knowing and keeping. When you want something bad enough and are willing to work hard, strength shows up. If you never try, never take a risk, you'll never know what is possible. Even when those closest to you place negative no-win ideas and fears of failure into your mind, your success can change them as much as it changes you. And we all began to grow closer.

Learning to drive helped. Not many people can function in this world without the ability to drive. Gram, a true exception, never learned. Grandpa had tried to teach her, but she drove into the ditch whenever an oncoming car approached. Grandpa gave up on her, but I didn't want to spend my life in the passenger seat.

Living so far away from school gave me miles of driving experience and hours of alone time with Grandpa once I had my driver's permit and license. Being with Grandpa in a closed space generated a bit of stress. I never saw him as much of a communicator, but I put on an interrogator hat and began probing into his life. Something amazing happened: he opened up and told me unbelievable things.

One time, he told me he went to a friend's house to fix his car, and when he got there the man's wife met him at the door, naked, and suggested a different kind of overhaul. Grandpa jumped in his own car and never went back. I often wondered if Gram knew these stories, but I never asked.

I learned that Grandpa suffered from migraine headaches. I always suspected the cause to be fumes from truck and car exhaust in the closed, poorly ventilated Ford garage where he worked. Unethical decisions and behaviors from the management team triggered migraines, too.

I remember one time he told me about a man from out of town who had been stranded and needed his car fixed so he could return to his family and job. Grandpa had ordered and received the parts and started to work on this man's car when his boss approached. "Hey Merv, stop working on that car. My friend needs a tune up so he can go on vacation. That other job can wait."

That night Grandpa came in the house, washed up with Lava soap, took an aspirin and an ice pack, closed the curtains, and went straight to bed without supper. He had been pulled off the job, and his boss lied to the out-of-towner, blaming no parts for the delayed service. Lies trigger pain.

Grandpa also told me about the Friday night infidelity game the managers at the garage played each week. They put their keys in a bowl, like Russian roulette, and each one picked up another man's keys and got his car and wife for the night. For several years Grandpa watched their infidelity and unethical behavior. Boy, how it bothered him.

Hearing these stories changed my view of my hard-working Grandpa. He was an ethical man with an eighth-grade education and higher standards than upper management. I began to see the man of my family and I was proud. Have you ever lost something you thought could never be found, only to open your eyes and heart and find it right in front of you? Grandpa, my grandpa, my hero, my friend will always be the best example of a family man named "Dad." He was a great mechanic who could fix anything broken, even me.

I got my driver's license when I was sixteen. Grandpa bought me a car, an old 1963 Mercury Monterey Breezeway with a middle rear window that could open and close. I loved every inch of that ivory-colored car, including the patched rust spots on the hood. I christened my rust bucket "Betsy." Grandpa kept her running like a Cadillac.

Grandpa and I became close by talking, laughing and storytelling. It's amazing how communication dissolves fear, nurtures trust, and plants an indescribable, mysterious, mutual love and respect. Our healthy grandfather-granddaughter relationship rose like baking powder biscuits in a hot gas oven. Grands, to be sure!

Patti and I became accustomed to the new-old way of living, and our relationship with Gram bloomed. I believe we helped her more than we burdened her. Our hearts softened when we realized she experienced sadness and heartache like anyone else. I remember one Mother's Day; she was sweeping the big oval brown braided rugs with a broom in the living room. She started to cry. I had never seen her cry. I put my arm around her shoulder and asked, "Grandma, what's wrong? Are you hurting somewhere? Why are you crying?"

Her answer startled me. "I miss my mother."

I didn't know how to respond to that. When I cried for Mom, Dad, Terry, or Lady, Gram's words of wisdom were, "Buck up. You're not the only kid whose parents got divorced." Sticking my grief in a pot with other kids from divorce I did not know didn't help me one bit. I could have spat those words back to Gram, but why top pain with spite?

I had never thought about Gram having a mother. I didn't know my great-grandmother. I handed Gram a tissue as she mopped tears between sobs. I stood quietly and let her miss her mom, and I cried with her. Gram had a heart. She had also hidden her special talents in the attic.

Every summer Patti, Gram, and I got up extra early on the day we did the one job that I detested, cleaning the attic. This adventure always fell on the hottest day of the year (not a great choice with no AC in any part of the house). Summer mustiness reigned.

After breakfast, we filed into the cramped bathroom and opened the white painted barn-like door across from the toilet. We scaled the steep steps to the attic by practically crawling upward. The attic ceiling sloped with the roof, so we carefully stooped over like the Hunchback of Notre Dame. Avoiding wasps and silverfish made my skin crawl and put me on edge at the sight of any tiny critter movement.

At the top of the stairs sat a bed without a headboard, dominating the first of the attic's two rooms. White painted shelves lined the wall to the second room. That was where Gram stored her "Grit" collection piles. After dusting the shelves and re-stacking the cherished newspapers, I made it into the back room to dust the chests of drawers. Curiosity struck and I peeked inside. "Gram what are these?"

As she made her way between the chests, she eyed the neatly folded cloth I had found in one of the drawers I had opened. "Oh, those are my quilt tops," she replied. "I have five, one for each of my grandchildren."

"Which one is mine?" I asked.

"The little Dutch girl"

"Okay Gram, you've been asking me what I want for high school graduation and now I know. I want my quilt."

"Put them back where you found them. We'll see about that."

High school prepares us for a major life change. Knowing I needed money for school, I quit cheerleading during my senior year to work at the custard stand at the only intersection in Sigel. This tiny town or village, complete with a general store, post office and custard stand, mirrored Mayberry. The owner of the custard stand and restaurant,

Flick Jolly, had been my mom's teacher in high school, and hired me. This job kick-started a career of taking requests, multi-tasking, and customer satisfaction.

Waitressing was more than taking orders from the dining room. Frozen, soft serve custard with weekly specialty flavors like tangerine, raspberry, and lemon drew customers for miles. The menu also included hot dogs, hamburgers, fries, hand-grated slaw, and a variety of meals. After ball games and school events, the custard machines struggled to keep up with orders. At times, people would have to wait or make another choice to allow time for their favorite mix to freeze.

A special skill set is needed to work in a custard stand. The ability to make a dip cone, for example, without the ice cream falling into the warm chocolate or caramel coating, is an art. Early in my new career, I also found milkshakes to be a considerable challenge even for the experienced worker.

One day, I slid open the glass window at the counter and asked, "How can I help you?"

The customer asked for "Three raspberry custard shakes, please."

"Okay, it will be just a minute."

I grabbed the boss's attention as he moved between flipping burgers and pouring frozen potatoes into the crackling-hot grease baskets. "Hey Flick, can you please help me? I need three raspberry shakes and I don't know how to make them."

Flick came out from behind the grill, wiped his hands on his grease-splattered apron, and lined up three cups. One at a time, he pulled up the silver lever of the custard machine and filled each cup three-quarters full of luscious loops of light purple raspberry custard. Tapping the cups hard on the counter, he grabbed milk from the refrigerator and sloshed in a hefty amount. Taking two of the cups in his big hands, he quickly jammed them up onto the milkshake maker and turned to me with a stern look. "Watch closely," he said, as if this moment in time represented my one and only training opportunity. As he gave each cup multiple squeezes, the spinner twirled the custard, whipping the milk right out of the cup and splashing a light purple mural onto the ceiling and walls and all over the counter. Furious, Flick snatched off his apron and began to sop up the explosive, sticky mess. Laughing uncontrollably, I couldn't help but ask, "So that's how it's done?" And I gathered up towels to help clean up the mess. I watched his angry glare snap to a smirk, turn to a smile, and then transform into a jelly-belly laugh. "No, that's not how it's done. You can learn a lot by knowing what not to do. Don't get into a hurry and don't add too much milk."

What a mess! It reminded me of Bill Jamison's wisdom after I had dropped those mashed potatoes on the living room floor. If this was the worst thing that could happen, we were going to make it. Flick's momentary glare didn't faze me. We both laughed. I helped clean up the mess and I made the shakes, always careful to add the milk gradually. The raspberry volcanic eruption makes me laugh to this day.

Chapter 7:

Hits to the Heart

I n my senior year of high school, I landed the role of Louise in the musical *Carousel*. I needed a costume, so I called Mom, my personal expert seamstress. I remembered how easily she had whipped up beautiful pink satin ballerina outfits, sporting rows of light pink, magenta and turquoise sequins secured with invisible lines of perfect handwork. Following rough sketches and crude instructions provided by my dance instructor, Arita Lee Blair, Mom had tamed miles of wild netting into perfectly balanced ruffled tutus. Making dresses for a musical would be sewing 101 compared to dance costumes. When Mom accepted the challenge, I was thrilled.

Knowing she crafted my dresses for the musical amplified my resolve to make her proud. Planning for graduation, memorizing lines and songs, and looking for next steps in life was a challenge. Sometimes things fall into place. Time off work, no problem. Mom in the audience with Grandma, Grandpa, and little sis? Wow, you couldn't have poured another drop of love and anticipation into my heart cup. My joy bubbled over—until the phone call came from Mom the night before the first show in May. "I'm so sorry," she said, "but I can't come to your musical. I shot off my mouth and Rip set me straight. I've got bruised ribs and a black eye, and I can't let your grandmother see me looking like this. Don't tell her. This is all my fault."

Mom always attached a note to anything she made by hand. It read: "There is love in every stitch." What does an abuser say about his handiwork? Love in every hit, you witch. He dealt it, Mom felt it, and this time, so did I.

The last song of the musical was mine. Songs pierce hearts when sung with conviction. Standing on stage and singing about dreams being tossed around during storms in life felt like a public confession of my disappointments. The music continued, and even though I had memorized the lyrics weeks before, it was on that night when the song's meaning sank into my soul. Hope. Keep hope. Keep your head up high. I knew deep inside that the only constant, the only one who could keep me from walking through this life alone and in despair, was God. He keeps promises. He is the hope I hold in my heart.

As I drove home from the performance in the dark, I decided that if I ever fell in love and got married, I would never get divorced. My children would never have to worry about broken promises. No man would ever abuse me or beat me. Love would rule my life. God would be the head of my family and we would never walk alone.

We celebrated my graduation party at home. Of course, Gram made my favorite meal: ham loaf, scalloped potatoes, slaw, succotash, homemade rolls, and lemon meringue pie. After we cleaned the dishes, the family gathered in the living room to watch me open my gifts. Grandpa sat cross legged on his recliner, grinning hugely as I opened his present first.

I cried. It was a King James Bible with giant print, just like his. I knew he had picked it out himself. He said, "I got to thinkin' of how much readin' you'll be doing, and I got the big print, so your eyes won't get tired." I hugged and thanked him.

Smiling, head cocked to the right, glasses perched low so her big brown eyes studied my face, Gram gingerly handed me the last gift. The box seemed way too small and light to hold a quilt. Disappointment ran through my mind, but for once my tongue stayed still and quiet as a sparrow aware it is in the sights of a Cooper's hawk.

Some days it's so great to be wrong, wrong, wrong! Why do I lean toward the negative impossibilities of life instead of believing anything is possible? I opened the gift to see my quilt, with its beautiful aqua, yellow, and pink little Dutch girls wearing bonnets, all so sweetly dressed in prints that Gram had painstakingly matched up. "How did you do it? Gram, it is lovely! I love my quilt. How did you keep this from me?"

With a big smile, Gram confessed, "After you girls jumped on the bus, I jumped into my high boots and walked back the Sharp Road to Ethel's. The quilt frame has been in her living room, and we worked on it together, every day or two this winter."

It must have taken amazing stamina for my little round Gram to walk at least a mile through Pennsylvania snow to give me what I wanted for graduation. Love in every stitch? Love in every step! There was also a gift from me to her: a newfound love of quilting. Once the quilt bug bit, Gram finished many more than the five from the attic.

The lessons Gram and Grandpa taught me over our five years together will never be found in any book or course. Making sauerkraut, apple sauce, and apple butter, gardening, identifying and nurturing every blossom God ever created, and being exposed to past ways of country life unknowingly prepared me for my future in nursing. Home-grown compassion for others was our way of life.

One of my best friends in high school had always wanted to be a nurse, so I decided it would be fun for us to take that journey together. Acceptance into a nursing school program opened an entire new chapter in my life, full of new friends, strict routines, communal living, and loads of fun, learning, and memory making. Sharon General Hospital School of Nursing, here I come!

Chapter 8:

She Thinks It's Blue

Sharon General Hospital School of Nursing, a three-year diploma school, was a few hours away from my grandparents' home, near the border of Pennsylvania and Ohio. I felt a bit abandoned and stranded. I stayed in the dorm attached to the hospital with about 130 girls, and on our floor, there was one hall phone. Girls ran to answer it on the first ring, picked up the receiver, and then screamed for Judy, Vicky, Laura Lou, or whoever. They seldom screamed for Donna.

Once, Gram did call, and I was so excited for a moment. "Donna," she said, "I'm calling to tell you Stanley Pierce from church died."

"Oh."

Gram kept it short. "Don't want the phone bill to be high. We thought you should know."

One time they called, and I got to talk with Grandpa. Excited about clinicals, I told him, "Grandpa, I gave my first shot today."

His response: "How did the patient take it?

"The shot was fine, but he did die two hours later."

Laughing, Grandpa said, "You will never give me a shot!"

47

Because I had no income and no way to pay for car insurance, my rust bucket, Betsy, stayed at Grandpa's. It really was more like a loaner. I did not have the freedom to drive home on the weekends, so I worked as a nurse aide.

In high school I had maintained As and Bs with ease. Nursing school expectations threw me into unfamiliar territory. I found myself struggling to achieve even a C in one of my first classes: Anatomy. Maintaining a high GPA was essential to success. If you got Cs or Ds, you got booted from the program.

I had two plans for dealing with this problem. For Plan A, I had to ensure that I had a place to go if the worst-case scenario came to fruition. I called Gram and asked, "If I fail nursing school can I come home?"

"No," she answered without hesitation. "We don't have room for you and all your stuff. Your old bedroom is a guest room now and I have my quilt up over the bed."

I've always heard it said that you can never go home again. It feels cruel and heartless when your family says it and means it. So much for Plan A.

My Plan B involved finding out from my professor what I could do to improve my grade. Just how far down into the pit of flunk had I fallen? I stayed after class one day to talk to my Ms. Anatomy, a retired military spinster whom I was terribly afraid of since my entire class had recently caused her red-faced fume.

Because there was a huge test scheduled for Nursing Fundamentals, we all chose to study for that test and opted not to read the anatomy assignment on the reproductive system. The minute we took our seats in Anatomy class that afternoon, our instructor said, "Class, take out a sheet of paper and on one side write everything you know about the female reproductive system and on the other side do the same for the male." The class gasped in unison; We were in deep doo-doo. The next day in class, after she reviewed our work, Ms. Anatomy blew a gasket.

"It's clear to me you students did not do your reading. Girls, you should be ashamed. I have read more about the penis than I ever care to. It's the only thing you have on your minds."

We had three male nursing students in our class and one whispered, "Don't worry girls, she thinks it's blue." Laughter erupted like a volcanic explosion; we couldn't hold back the giggles, snorts, belly shakes, and tears. In the textbook the diagram of male private parts was pale blue. Volcanic ash from our eruption of amusement must have hit Ms. Anatomy. "And you think this is funny? I want all of you to review the models of the male and female pelvis until you identify the parts by heart."

There I was, waiting in my seat after class, needing advice from someone so recently offended. And yes, I confess, I did laugh. When the room cleared, I mustered some courage. "Ms. A. do you have time to talk with me?"

"Sure."

"I believe I am going to fail. As you know, I received the lowest C and lowest D on my last two exams. I never got such bad grades in high school and I don't think I've got what it takes to be a nurse. Do you think I should quit nursing school?"

With a look of calm concern, she took a seat in the row in front of me. She must surely have seen the surface tension of my juicy eyes reaching the dripping point. "Donna," she told me, "I would rather be cared for by a C-average nurse who personifies kindness, compassion, and common sense than an RN who maintains a 4.0 average, any day. Keep trying, you have time to improve your grade. Don't quit."

And I stayed.

Little did I know that spending the first day of deer season with Grandpa a year ago had given me skills to pass this class. Nothing could stop Grandpa from getting his buck, not even an elbow abscess from a metal shard. I had received specific instructions the night before. "Eat your breakfast, get dressed, be ready to head down to the natural gas pipelines behind Bill's and help me drag the deer out of the woods. I'll be calling you around 7:10."

Next morning, while I was still in my PJs and eating toast and drippy eggs, the phone rang at the promised time. Uh-oh! I flew. I dressed as fast as possible in boots, suspender snow pants, jacket, hood, gloves, and scarf to crunch through the eight-inch crusty snow. I trudged for a half mile to the pipeline. Grandpa, proud and smiling, had already gutted the six-point buck. Obediently, I took hold of the antlers on the right side while Grandpa proceeded to slide the deer over the snow with his good arm. I ambled clumsily along with him, trying hard to keep up and not fall. At our garage, we hoisted the deer up with a pulley and Grandpa said, "Here is where I really need your help. I have to slice the facia and skin the deer and you have to pull down on the hide." I did as he said, and together we skinned that deer with ease.

The day Ms. A. distributed big, clear, stinky body baggies and scalpels for our lesson on skinning, dissecting, and identifying muscles, tendons, bones, and ligaments, many of my classmates turned green. Ms. A. gave the sacrificial speech: "These cats have given their lives for you…"

What an unbelievable stench of formaldehyde arose from the fur of the martyrs! Once the fur was removed from the cats the odor became much more tolerable. Zip, zap, zip! I skinned my cat in record time. Thank you, Grandpa! Many of my cat-loving friends struggled. Holding your nose and trying to breathe while wielding a scalpel handicaps any skinner.

My maiden name was Mushrush, and all through high school and nursing school my peers and instructors used my nickname. "Mush, how did you do that so quickly? Would you, could you please skin my cat for me?"

My answer: "Of course I will help you. I once helped Grandpa skin a deer." I thanked God for an elbow abscess, and I helped skin multiple cats for my friends.

My grades improved. I made a B, didn't flunk out, and placed the kind and encouraging words of Ms. Anatomy in a special compartment of my memory bank. Improvement takes time. If you choose to quit, the clock stops. Time's chance to change is gone.

Chapter 9:

Giant Adventures

Nursing school exposed me to amazing people and experiences. My psychiatric clinical rotation made unforgettable memories. On my first day in the locked unit, our instructor sat at the head of the table in the conference room surrounded by ten fearlings. Sets of frog eyes, straight lip lines, ears stuck in listening mode, arms held tightly across our waists like straitjackets, racing hearts, and clammy clenched palms were probably normal student nurse reactions to the psych ward.

Every day at 10:00 a.m., patient families gathered outside the heavy locked doors for visiting hours. To ensure safety and prevent anyone from escaping, all patients knew to retreat to their rooms. One six-foot seven-inch, 320-pound resident refused to go back to his room. Standing a few feet away from the security doors, he called out to his wife: "Honey, I can't wait to see you." The nurse manager called security.

Security did not inspire in us any sense of safety or relief. The guard's attire was appropriate, but his stature was not; he was only four feet tall. A real-life David and Goliath encounter ensued. He stood there in front of the patient with his hands deep in his navy jacket pockets, name badge in view, eyes and head down, voice low and monotone. A pathetic negotiation ensued.

The guard cowered as the distressed patient towered over him. Every word shot from the little guy's rhetorical sling was countered by the tall patient's unwavering determination. Their parley went a little like this:

Guard: "You better go back to your room."

Patient: "I want my wife."

Guard: "Go back to your room."

Patient: "Honey, are you out there?"

Guard: "I think it would be a good idea if you go back to your room."

Patient: "Not without my wife."

Guard: "Go back to your room and we will bring your wife to you."

Patient: "Honey, get back away from the door. I'm coming to get you."

It was like a scene from a romantic movie. Goliath took several steps back and, eyes focused with laser accuracy on the center of the door, he began an approach to the long jump that would have done Jesse Owens proud. After several floor-shaking steps, he leapt high in the air with the grace of an elephant ballerina, using his feet like a battering ram against the thick security doors. The doors flew open, their glass fractured, and Goliath landed safely. Then, with utmost tenderness, he took the hand of his wife and calmly walked without hesitation back to his room.

Our instructor quickly led us out of the newly unlocked psych unit. Our major concern, in the wake of this incident, was "And just how many weeks do we have to come here?"

Security processes carry great intent, but one can never dismiss the power of human interaction, creative communication, adrenalin, and the will of Goliath.

Walking was a great form of exercise and my only means of transportation while at Sharon, PA. When a group of us were off on Sundays, we rotated to different churches for worship. On one of those Sunday mornings, a group of us were going to attend mass when we ran into a confused patient from a nearby nursing home walking down the middle of the road, looking terribly lost with her windblown hair and blue and white nightgown. Happy to see us, she grabbed onto the nearest hand and begged for help in a thick Italian accent. "I am looking for America," she said." Can you girls help me find it?"

Red-headed Lynn quickly answered, "But of course, walk with us and we will take you there." We all knew Elisabetta. Our nursing home rotation had given us the opportunity to care for her and the many residents diagnosed with organic brain syndrome.

That morning, we lied to a poor lost soul on our way to church. The nursing staff thanked us when we returned her to the home, but not Elisabetta. She sadly shook her head and her finger at all of us, saying "This is not America. I want to go to America." She cried as we abandoned her in the foreign country known as the Old Folks Home.

On Saturday nights, I loved to go dancing with my friends. They loved me too, for I drank water and Coke and proudly held the designated driver label. One night, Lynn drove us to the dance hall. Around 2:00 a.m., like sardines, more girls than seats piled into the tiny red car and I slid into the driver's seat, put the keys in the ignition, and gasped.

A manual transmission? East State Street morphed into an insurmountable peak. Imagine drunken friends cracking up with every jerk or stall. Miraculously, there were no injuries, no tickets, and no need to call for ralph. After this escapade, I scribbled a new entry on my list of things to do someday: learn to drive stick.

In my senior year of nursing school our class broke up into three groups of fifteen students for the last semester. Our pediatric rotation sent us to the Cincinnati Children's Hospital in Ohio. Of all my clinical rotations, this one won the award for being terribly stressful. Major organizational changes had given the Ohio nurses bitter attitudes and no desire to teach newbies. If my memory serves me right, I believe a strike or a partial shutdown was already brewing when we arrived.

My nursing instructor there infuriated me. I seldom saw him, and once when I did, I told him I needed help and got very little for my trouble. The hair of the little black girl I was assigned to care for was sticking straight up in the air, so I asked him, "Can you please tell me how to braid black hair?" His response: "Well, I can see you didn't do your homework. Once you knew the assignment, you should have found out how to care for her hair. You're on your own." Then he quickly stormed down the hall. That was frustrating enough, but it wasn't the only thing I needed to ask.

Child abuse is an ugly thing. Someone had put this poor baby's hands in a pot of boiling water. It was unbelievable to me to see the results of such cruelty. Healing happened over the last few weeks. Eventually no more dressings or Silvadene were necessary as her skin, at last pink and intact, allowed her to do toddler things like eat with her hands. She did an amazing job with her spaghetti noodles. Cleanup for me was a challenge, as her enthusiasm about the spaghetti left orange spaghetti sauce all over her face and those little hands. I removed her tray, scooped up all the noodles, washed her face and came up with the stupidest idea I have ever had.

I took a towel, a washcloth, and a bowl of cool soapy water and set them down on her highchair tray, thinking she could splash the bubbles as I cleaned her hands. I never saw true terror come over anyone until that moment.

Her eyes were wide, her breathing deep and rapid, and her eardrum-bursting screams threw me into action. I put the bowl on the floor, covered it with the towel, grabbed her up out of the highchair and repeated, "No, no, no sweetheart. It's okay. I'm not going to hurt you. I would never hurt you." I carried her to a nearby rocking chair and snuggled her tight while we cried. She fell asleep in my arms, and I prayed, "Oh dear God forgive me, she thought I was going to scald her." I rocked and prayed for safety for this baby. Child protective services would place her.

Later that afternoon, her Gamma came, laid my little one across her knees, and used hair gel to smooth and cornrow that wild head of hair. At the end of my shift, my toddler smiled and said, "Bye, Bye, Wuv you." Her name was Precious.

Another evening on the cancer unit a nurse announced in disgust, "Kid wants someone to pray with him. I'm not doing it. Anyone here know how to pray?" I volunteered. "Sure, I'll be happy to. What room?"

"Nine."

I went into room nine to find a young boy snuggled under white sheets with a fuzzy blanket from home and a soft brown stuffed dog.

"Hi," I said, giving him a warm smile. "What's your name?"

"Tommy."

"I'm Donna. I understand you want someone to say prayers with you before you go to sleep. I'd be happy to do that. Can I sit on the bed beside you?"

"Sure."

"Tell me Tommy, how do you pray with your mommy and daddy? Do you have a special prayer or do you make them up as you go?"

"Oh, I just talk to God like I talk to you."

"Do you want me to just listen and hold your hand, or would you like me to pray too when you finish?"

"Yes, that would be fine."

And I listened to a sick little 8-year-old praying for safety and health for his parents and four brothers and sisters by name. His thank you list included the simple things we take for granted. "Lord, thank you for my matchbox cars. You know how much I love my red Camaro. And thank you when little sissy fell off the slickly slide last week, she only got a little bump on her knee." A child's prayer is simple, sweet, sincere, and saturated in total belief that the Lord hears every word.

My turn came and I thanked God for letting me meet Tommy and I asked for healing. We said our goodbyes, and he thanked me with a hug.

A sad thought hit as I left his room: I won't be here again. My rotation was complete. What if no one is willing to pray? Then again, if God sent me, He can send someone tomorrow, maybe Tommy's mom or dad.

Our Cincinnati pediatric rotation ended, and we returned home. Sharon, Pennsylvania never looked so good. The last semester of our senior year overflowed with hard choices that threatened even the healthiest family relationships I knew. Graduating from a teenage granddaughter to an independent young woman, a nurse with endless opportunities, ignited hot, searing, uncontrollable Mervin Cowan anger. Nothing in life prepared me for this.

Chapter 10:

Transitions

Anger, like a prickly weed with hidden sharp thorns, pops up in the garden of life and tears the most protective coat or skin. Whether you're thick- or thin-skinned, anger stings just the same. I take responsibility. My life choices made my grandparents livid.

All nursing seniors received a thick catalog of hospitals from all over the United States. I sifted through those pages with passion, pondering benefits and salaries. A Michigan hospital got my attention, but North Carolina seemed to be calling me. My book kept falling open to a university medical center in Durham. I loved the majestic look of the hospital, the ecumenical Christian chapel, the great restaurants, the dinner theatres, and the fact the ocean was only a few hours away.

When I broke the news to my grandparents that I would be moving to Durham, they came unglued, especially Grandpa. He yelled at me while he paced furiously back in forth in the living room. I shook inside and out. I couldn't wait to get away from the insensitive words Grandpa spat at me.

"You don't know nothing about paying bills. You don't know nothing about money. And you want to move where? You don't know anyone in North Carolina."

I held back the tears as I took the verbal beating. Then I sighed, shook my head, and retreated to my bedroom. I knew exactly what they wanted me to do. They imagined me living in a mobile home in the field above the garden and getting a job at the local hospital. Like a chameleon, my mood changed from compliant to stubborn and rebellious the more I thought about it.

After the blowup about my choice to go to North Carolina, I didn't go home much for the remainder of my senior year. I called Mom and Rip, and they took me to Durham for my interview. I got the job on the spot, put down a deposit on an apartment about eight minutes from the hospital, and returned to finish the last month of school in the spring of 1978. My grandparents and I did not speak. The bitter silent treatment went on for months. German pride often involves traipsing through life under a negative umbrella paired with emotions like stubbornness or self-ishness. But pride can also be the catalyst to repair relationships, at least in my family.

One afternoon the dorm phone rang, and a friend yelled, "Mush, it's for you." Gram broke the wall of silence. Like a journalist, she sought specific details for a writeup about my new job in the local paper. "Now, Donna, how do you spell that city in North Carolina? It is Duke University you will be working at?"

"Yes, Gram. I will be starting my job in June. I've accepted a position on Strudwick ward, named after a physician. I'll be living in Durham, North Carolina. I'll probably catch a Southern drawl."

Gram sent me copies of the article and underlined the most important phrase several times with her pen: "the granddaughter of Dorothy and Mervin Cowan." Pride helped heal our relationship, along with a surprise visit.

My brother drove from Pennsylvania to North Carolina to deliver my few belongings in his big navy-blue van with a helper in the passenger seat: Grandpa. They drove over five hundred miles to carry furniture, hang pictures, and check the locks on the only door of my upstairs apartment. I don't believe either of my grandparents had ever driven more than two hours from home in all the years I lived with them.

Terry pulled up to my apartment and I was running to hug him when I saw the passenger door open. Out stepped a grand surprise: Grandpa! I had no idea he was coming. I threw my arms around him and hugged him hard. "It's so good to see you, Grandpa. What a surprise this is for me!" And he grinned and patted my back. Then the two best men in my life got to work unloading my cedar hope chest and belongings.

Before they left to return to Pennsylvania, I drove Grandpa all over Durham to specific places. He needed to see the laundromat, the grocery stores, the hospital, the gas station, and the bank. My safety mattered to him. I mattered. My brother and my grandpa loved me.

My Duke days began. My first job required new graduates to work all three shifts in a ten-day stretch. We started with four day shifts, then worked three evenings and always ended the stretch with three nights. My sleep schedule got crazy and I felt horrible. I could never plan anything.

When orientation was completed, I transferred to the only permanent shift, available, nights. I worked Sunday through Thursday from 11:00 p.m. until 7:00 a.m. I was the only RN on night shift, and I worked with an LPN and a nurse aide. I arrived at 10:00 p.m., off the clock, and poured my medications into little white paper cups with cards bearing patient room numbers and names. At 11:00 p.m. I went to the conference room and received an oral report from the evening shift nurse on all forty patients on the ward.

The experiences I had on the night shift are etched forever in my memory bank. One night during rounds an elderly female patient went missing. I found her in bed with a man four rooms down the hall. "Oh Marilyn," I told her, "You need to go back to your own room."

Sheepishly, she wiggled out from under the covers, pulled down her hospital gown, shrugged her shoulders, and with a giggling whisper said, "Sorry, hope we didn't wake anyone. We tried to be quiet."

"Marilyn, how long have you known that man?"

"To be honest, we just met tonight." And back to her own room we walked.

Documentation of patient vital signs recorded by the nurse's aide was my responsibility, and it was also a problem. One time, alarmed, I approached Ms. Aide and asked, "How can everyone down the hall have a blood pressure of 90/60?" Her southern drawl and lackadaisical attitude floored me as she answered, "Just tis so. I'm goin' on break now." And I retook everyone's vital signs. I reported this event to my manager, Nancy. She loved Ms. Aide, a loyal employee, and she did not investigate the matter. My gut told me something was not right, and I watched my aide closely.

The last three beds at the end of our hall made up the trauma unit. A male patient tried to commit suicide—he took a gun to his head and miraculously missed every vital element of his brain. Ms. Aide heard about him during report, sashayed to his bedside, and blurted, "If you were depressed before you tried to blow your brains out, you gotta be more depressed now. You can't even kill yourself right." And then she cackled so loud and hard, people ran down the hall and into the room to see a hysterical aide hovering over a sobbing middle-aged man. Boss Nancy chose to do nothing.

I spoke to the night shift director of nursing about my concerns, only to find my aide's family had contacted Nancy asking if her co-workers had noticed any bizarre behavior. They were greatly concerned and checked her into a mental hospital for evaluation. Ms. Aide checked herself out against medical advice and was scheduled to work every night for the next month.

The night shift director of nursing encouraged me to leave my unit, for patient safety fell upon my shoulders, which made Ms. Aide's behavior my responsibility. It isn't humanly possible to become someone's shadow. I took the director's advice and put in a transfer to the trauma unit for fear of losing my license. Ms. Nancy held me on the unit for twelve weeks and never spoke another word to me.

Early in my nursing career I learned my family didn't hold the patent on the silent treatment when offended. Much to my dismay and disappointment dysfunctional walls of silence can be easily built by work families. Even those in healthcare.

Chapter 11:

The Big Fisherman

At age twenty, I developed keen money management skills despite making only $4.95 an hour. Grandpa's voice echoed in my head: "Never buy anything you don't have the money to pay for." Little did he know, he taught me to live by a rare and successful principle of finance—learn to do without. By the time I paid for my rent, electricity, car payment, insurance, groceries, and gasoline, I had a bit left over. I celebrated by buying a few things for my apartment. My first spending spree included a toilet brush and toilet bowel cleaner.

I loved living in the south. If you are ever on the receiving end of a scoop of that hospitality, you never forget it. The day before Thanksgiving, as I was standing at the nursing station, one of my black co-workers asked, "Are you going home for the holidays?"

"No Nan, I don't have enough days off to get to Pennsylvania. I'll get a little turkey and be fine."

Nan moved closer, put her right hand on her hip and wagged her diamond-clad fingers in front of my face. "No child you will not. You are coming to my house." Penning down her phone number and address on the corner of a report sheet, she jammed it in my hand. "And don't you be late now. Brunch starts at 11:00 a.m. sharp and I'm not taking no. You best be there."

Thanksgiving morning, her husband greeted me at the door and asked what I wanted to drink. Stupid me, I said, "Oh anything." He hurried about fixing me something that resembled green soap suds with a nasty taste, probably alcohol. I sat the drink on a coaster by a plant after a tiny sip. Nan rescued me by taking me on a tour of her house.

In the hallway an entire wall, top to bottom, held the greatest attraction: A photo array of love. Nan proudly introduced me to all of her framed foster children, all sixteen of them, at various phases of their lives. Many grew up and joined the military. They were all beautiful, with captivating smiles. Even though a picture hangs still, their looks of love moved me. What a family! What a life legacy!

The doorbell rang, and in came her church family. We laughed, talked, and carried on a bit, and I savored sweet potato pie. I felt so special. I remembered an old hymn from church entitled "He included me. When my Lord said whosoever, He included me." Nan included me. That night I went to bed filled with thanks and full to the brim. Nan shared a true Thanksgiving with her black family and one single little white girl.

Tight friendships grew in Durham like butterbeans in the red earth. I enjoyed my work family and my friends in the apartment complex. But I did have struggles with my new life of independence. Each of us can wander like the prodigal son. Some run wild. Some run so far away, fueled with bitterness, that they never come home. Some run away from God. I was more like a fish than a runner.

I imagine the heavenly Father as my big fly fisherman. He casts the line baited with the fly he tied. I get hooked and struggle, but He takes His time and reels me in, pulling me out of my sin stream with a net, and gives me a choice: stay with Him or jump back into the stream and go it alone. If you choose the Fisherman, He will equip you to be a fisher of men.

When I realized I never wanted to be out of God's reach, I broke off unhealthy relationships, went to church, attended Bible studies, and joined a Christian book club. Like a person who hadn't eaten a good meal in years, I couldn't get enough. I buried my head in my hands, knelt, and prayed daily in the brown and rust rocker in the living room. Several strange things happened.

While I prepared for work one night, someone knocked on my door. When I opened it, my friend David stood there, hands in his jean pockets, with a peculiar half smile on his face as he stammered, "Uh, Donna. I need your help. You know how much I love Paula. You see I've asked her to marry me and she won't until I become a Christian. Can you tell me how to do that?"

"Oh yeah. Come on in. I just need to make a phone call." I called work and let them know I might be a bit late. I usually arrived early, worked extra when they needed me, and never requested anything. My manager's reply: "No problem. Our census is low, get here when you can."

Another time, on my day off, I received a telephone call. "Hello! Is this Donna Mushrush?"

"Yes, this is Donna."

"Well, you don't know me," he said, snickering, and I wondered if this was to be an obscene phone call. "I'm Russ and I play drums in a Christian Band. We're looking for a female vocalist and a friend of mine told me to call you. Want to schedule an audition?"

Perplexed, I thought, why not? I scheduled an audition for the following Saturday morning. All week I thought about the audition and what opportunities might lie ahead.

Saturday came. I followed the directions to a lovely home, knocked on the door and met Geri, the wife of the band leader. She escorted me to the basement. Or, rather, the recording studio, set up with a true sound booth and mixer. I met Bruce, the band leader, Russ, the drummer, and

Evan, the bass player. Geri played the piano, and they taught me one of their original songs: "You loved me."

It was quite an unexpected experience, with a great group of personality-packed people. They thanked me for coming, and on the drive home I asked God, "How and why is this happening? That was so cool." An old, old memory popped to the front of my mind. Sometime in my young life I attended a youth camp. We slept on the floor on lumpy mattresses and sleeping bags. One night my friends and I stood about two rows from the Christian band during the worship service. It was the first time I had ever experienced singing and praising God with drums, guitars, a keyboard, and singers. I said to myself, "Wow, how I would love to sing in a band like that someday."

A favorite Psalm of mine says, "…And he will give you the desires of your heart." As I fumbled to unlock the door to my apartment, with my camp memory still in mind, I could hear the phone ringing. I bolted in and grabbed the receiver, only to hear Russ: "Hey there Donna. It's Russ. Welcome to our Christian Band."

"Lord, really? The desires of my heart even twelve to fifteen years later? Thank you so much."

My Duke days hold some of my most precious memories. Education thrived. Physicians respected nurses. I achieved my certification in critical care, worked in multiple ICUs, and even had the opportunity to dive in the hyperbaric chamber. I worked with nurses from all over the United States.

In 1981, I decided to move to the Midwest to be close to my brother. His life had hit a rough spot, and I wanted to be there for him as he always had been for me.

Evansville, Indiana is where I met Bill McCutchan, and a new chapter of choices began.

Chapter 12:

Plug In

I n my experience, choosing to move is a source of wild energy and excitement despite the work; it's a complete turnabout from the dark cloud of dread that hovers over a forced move. Sorting, tossing, packing and unpacking, organizing, and arranging can actually be enjoyable. Saying goodbye to roommates, neighbors, and friends carries some sadness, but the chance to live with my big brother for a season felt right.

The trip from North Carolina to Indiana seemed perfect until the movers delivered the furniture. My hope chest, table and chairs, bedroom set, stereo cabinet all survived the move without a scratch, but my Lowry organ didn't. Ever since I was a kid, I had always wanted to play piano or organ. I used to pluck the keys and try to teach myself how to play on Mom's old pale blue speckled upright. I came home from school one day and it was gone.

The morning the repair man assessed the situation with my poor Lowry, I paced between the kitchen and family room awaiting a costly and possible fatal diagnosis. After a few minutes he announced "Lady, this is the easiest sixty-five dollars I've ever made. Your organ is fine. You just forgot to plug it in."

Laughing at my own stupidity, I wrote a check.

To start a new life in a different city, I needed to plug into a work and church family and adjust to living with my big brother—the priceless member of my broken family. When my resume hit the human resource departments of the three hospitals, I became more like the hunted than the hunter. The experience and education I had gleaned from working at Duke University for three and a half years—from 1978 to 1981—set me up for success. I received several great offers and accepted a job in an ICU/Trauma unit. Being wanted is an amazing feeling. Within a few months I found a strong Bible-teaching church with a great choir and an adult singles group. Friendships developed quickly.

I loved living with Terry. His house sat on a hill within walking distance of the zoo, and often visitors traipsed about in the backyard. Strange, screechy, high-pitched noises alerted us to walk out back and enjoy the beauty of the majestic peacocks. Nothing stirs wonder like watching the long trail of a tail transform into an iridescent feathery fan of blue and green lace to grab a female peacock's attention.

The zoo manager lived down the street from us, and Terry had befriended him. This provided us with free manure for the garden. The biggest I'd ever seen. Terry kidded and said, "Big manure will give us big vegetables." In reality, it seemed to create an obstacle course for us as we hoed the green beans while maneuvering around the elephant doo-doo balls.

Terry worked during the day and took night classes; he was working on an industrial engineering degree. He encouraged me to take extra classes for college credit, since I only had a diploma in nursing, so I enrolled. My schedule was the opposite of Terry's. I worked nights, took morning classes, and slept during the day. I enjoyed the work-school life and took communications classes at the University of Evansville over the summer of 1981.

I lived with my brother for several months, and then eventually joined two of my friends, Robin and Kathy, to rent a house together.

It was a three-bedroom red-brick ranch on a dead-end road, just a few minutes from the hospital, and it was perfect. Of course, a clothesline and garden spot pulled my heart strings. Another sweet part of this rental agreement was that our landlords lived right next door. Anyone who knew Linda and John Bush loved them. She was a great cook and John could fix anything. They were loving Christian friends from church. In many ways we all became an extended family.

Robin, Kathy, and I often attended the adult singles group on Tuesday nights at the Christian Fellowship non-denominational church. The singles group helped us all to develop a stronger Christian walk, and it gave everyone an opportunity to know each other on a deep level. It was a safe, non-threatening way to develop lasting friendships with both sexes. We gathered in a room above the gymnasium. Pastor Steve set us up with interactive role play, lively table discussions, or an in-depth Bible study that was always framed neatly with a message to apply to our lives once we left. We shared prayer concerns every week in different ways. One evening we wrote our anonymous concerns on index cards and tossed them in a basket. We were then instructed to take a concern home (making sure not to take your own) and tape it to your bathroom mirror as a reminder. We often broke off into groups afterwards and shared drinks and snacks of cookies, relish, and sometimes sandwiches.

The singles group, like our Bible-teaching church, kept growing. New people showed up frequently. Some came seeking spiritual growth and comradery, others came seeking someone to date. One Tuesday night, I noticed a man I'd never seen before. He was clean shaven, with his sandy hair perfectly parted to the right, smartly dressed with a brown leather jacket under his arm. He came up to me and asked, "Do you happen to know what kind of cookies these are?"

"Sure do." I said, walking beside him as I pointed out the various types. "I made the gingersnaps. They were Grandpa's favorite. Kathy made the peanut butter and chocolate chips." He grabbed a bottle of water and invited me to sit with him. He led us to a table near the far wall.

In a formal manner, he extended his right hand and said, "I'm Bill McCutchan."

I smiled and responded, "Nice to meet you, my name is Donna, Donna Mushrush."

He gasped and nearly choked on his chocolate chip cookie. His laughter overcame all formality. "What? What kind of name is that?"

"My family is German, Pennsylvania Dutch, and some of the lineage goes back to Alsace-Lorraine France." I grinned. "And what about McCutchan? Did your family settle in McCutchanville?"

Bill gave me a brief history lesson on the McCutchanville settlers. The singles crowd thinned, and cleanup began. I needed to get home. Bill asked me for my phone number, and we made plans to go out for lunch the following Saturday.

When the word got out that I was going on a date with a stranger, my friends reminded me that looks can be deceiving. I heard stories of clean-cut men who charmed innocent women to death, like Ted Bundy. I told my friends, "You have watched way too many documentaries." And I told them to call the police if I didn't get home by 11:00 p.m. I felt they were a bit overly concerned, but naivety is one of my characteristics. I look for the good in people like Pollyanna.

On the day of our date, Bill picked me up and took me to the Evansville Country Club Grill for lunch. Over salads, cheeseburgers, and fries, I learned about the life of Bill McCutchan. He had attended Indiana University and worked as a loan officer for Old National Bank. He had one sister who lived in Indianapolis. His father was Harold O. McCutchan, a self-made man who came from nothing to become chairman of the board at Mead Johnson and Co. His millionaire father, now retired, had led the company in acquiring new drugs and the production and distribution of baby formula and nutritional supplements. When he spoke about his dad, a misty look of undeniable admiration came over Bill's face. He covered his dad's life story in explicit detail from stoking a coal stove as a boy in Chaffee, Missouri, through the divorce from his first alcoholic wife, and ultimately to the triumphant marriage to Bill's mother, Carol, who made H.O. the happiest man in the world.

Bill sipped long island teas between stories while I drank my water and lemon. I asked, "Bill what is in that tea?"

"Triple sec, vodka, tequila, rum, gin and Coke. Do you want to try one?"

"No, I've never been one who drank much," I told him, shaking my head with my hand on my mouth. "I was always the designated driver in nursing school. A glass of wine makes me loopy and I don't care much for that feeling."

He signed the bill and off we went. I thought we were heading home, but then he pulled into a parking lot and stopped the car. Reaching across me, he opened the glove box and grabbed a gun and a box of ammunition. My heart stopped. Could my friends have been right?

Tossing his head toward the building like a signal, he said, "Come on, this is a shooting range. I'll teach you to shoot. This will be fun."

I just sat there until Bill opened my car door and said, "Hey, it's okay. I have a permit, and this is legal."

It was a first date for the records: learning gun safety with a Smith and Wesson, donning earmuffs, and taking aim at a bullseye with Bill's arms around me as he tried to help me steady the gun. He was right—it was fun!

We dated for several months. In time, I met his family, attended parties, and dined with Bill at fancy restaurants. Then, just when I felt safe in our relationship, Bill pulled the plug.

Chapter 13:

Living in Limbo

My favorite communication principle is "No communication is communication." I love it because it's true. Bill stopped calling. No communication screamed, "I'm not interested in you." I found that hard to believe and became a telephone stalker. I broke a personal rule, not to call guys. I even called him at work, and he didn't take my calls. I stopped dialing.

Distressed and sad, I fell apart during my annual physical. Dr. Judy had asked me multiple questions about my family and personal life, and like a broken faucet, once I started crying, I couldn't stop. Trying to get to the root cause of my sadness, he asked me "Why are you crying?" I couldn't answer. Truth is, I didn't know. He wrote me a prescription for an anti-depressant that I filled but didn't use; I took one pill and threw the rest away. A few days later Dr. Judy called to check on me.

He was livid. "What do you mean you threw your pills away? I'm the physician here and you are definitely depressed about something."

"Dr. Judy," I said, "you hardly know me. You never considered I work nights and mandatory overtime. I work in the CCU, deal with codes, death, and open-heart transports. You never asked if I am exercising, eating right, or taking vitamins. I feel like a pill may be a last resort, not the first."

Finally, he said, "Okay here's what I want you to do." His voice was calm, and his words were carefully measured. "Get the military exercise manual from the library and create a personal exercise program. Try to see if you can transfer to a different unit and get on day shift. Step away from the ICU and come and see me in three months. Does that sound reasonable?"

And I agreed. I transferred to Same Day Surgery, which also meant I had to do some night and weekend call for the Recovery Room, but I did have more weekends off. I joined the YWCA and began water aerobics, continued going to church, and enjoyed my friends. I kept busy, mowing the yard, planting a garden, canning green beans. I buried my dreams of becoming a McCutchan, until one night when the phone rang and Kathy yelled for me. Covering the phone with her hand, she winked and whispered, "I think it's Bill."

"Hello?" I said.

"Um Donna, it's Bill. I just got a call from Mom. She's called 911 and they're taking Dad to the ER. Can I pick you up? I mean…could you please go with me?"

Without hesitating, I said, "Sure. What time will you be here?"

"About twenty minutes."

"I'll see you then." And like a quick-change artist, I was ready to go with minutes to spare.

Bill drove up in his big yellow Pontiac Grand Prix, and the moment I got in the car he thanked me over and over again. The little pine tree air freshener swinging on the radio nob gave off more than Bill's favorite clean car fragrance. The tree became a red flag. Any time we went out on a special date, Bill always cleaned the car, so I asked, "Did you do something special tonight?"

"Yes," he said. "If you've been wondering why I haven't been calling you it's Aunt Bettye. She's been hounding me to date other people, and I caved. You know how Aunt Bettye loves high society people with great reputations. Tonight, I took Shannon, one of the local news reporters, to the Kennel Club for dinner."

"Oh, I wondered why I hadn't heard from you. I hope you are enjoying yourself. I've seen her on TV, and she seems very nice."

"Well, she is, but…" He reached for my hand and squeezed it gently. "When this emergency with Dad came up, I only wanted you with me."

The ER staff took us to his dad's room and Bill hugged his mom. She thanked me for coming. They had sent his father out for tests, and because there were only two chairs in his room, I left Bill and his mother there and went to the waiting room in the lobby. As I waited, I thought about my past few weeks of wondering. Why the silence? My friend Robin had taken a risk and shared an honest assessment of Bill with me while I struggled with his absence. "Donna, I'm not sure he is right for you. Seems a negative root lives inside him. Sometimes he's not nice to you. He came to singles group one night and hasn't been back. I don't have a good feeling about him."

I suppose his Aunt Bettye probably had the same thoughts about me. Do other people have that much power over him? Can Bill really be so easily persuaded? Especially by someone like Bettye? I never knew anyone like her. I always try to find some positive attributes in people. Hers had to be balance and consistency. She balanced a cigarette and a highball glass in her long, pointy fingers while cigarette smoke and gossip swirled out of her pursed mouth. She plastered rich friends and acquaintances with arrogant judgments. She compared their scant donations to their net worth and shuddered as if it were a personal insult. She hated me for my faith. She often spouted, "Christians are weak, spineless creatures who believe in the myth of Jesus Christ."

I dreaded going to dinner at Aunt Bettye's, but that night sitting in ER, I realized she dreaded the thought of me being a part of the McCutchan family much more.

After three hours, Harold was discharged. He was diagnosed with diverticulitis, provided prescriptions and a list of food restrictions, and encouraged to rest. It was about 10:00 p.m. when we left the ER. Bill drove his parents home in their car and I followed in his Pontiac. The four of us settled in the cozy sitting room, with shelves stuffed with books to the ceiling, a brick fireplace, and large windows with café-style wooden shutters. We chatted a bit, drank a warm cup of cocoa, and then called it a night. Everyone was tired and grateful for a good outcome.

Bill opened up to me that night and told me know much I meant to him. He walked me to the door of my house and kissed me good night. From then on, we spent as much time together as possible. When we started dating seriously, some of the guys from the singles group began to let me know they were interested in me, too. I turned a blind eye, let them down easy, and stayed true to Bill.

One Saturday we drove to New Harmony, and Bill seemed nervous. We sat on a bench, and he reached into his jacket pocket and took out a three-page hand-written letter, which he read to me. It was one of the most beautifully written essays, full of his hopes and dreams in life, and it ended with his decision not to go it alone anymore. Then he proposed, and I said "yes" while he placed the prettiest white diamond engagement ring on my hand.

We then went to his parents' house and interrupted their evening. His dad glanced up from his paper and smiled, saying "I'm not surprised. Just amazed it took you so long, Bill." His mother congratulated me and asked us all to go to the sitting room. Once there, we shared celebratory drinks—brandy for Bill and Harold, wine coolers for Carol and me.

Carol, true to the character I would come to know all too well, said "Well, we need to discuss what you will call us now that you are engaged. You will call me Mrs. McCutchan and H.O., Mr. McCutchan."

At this, Harold reared up and said, "Aw honey, I don't care what you call me." Flustered by his non-supportive response, she shot him the evil eye and cried out, "Harold!", and I witnessed the executive of one of the largest pharmaceutical companies in the country agree to the put-and-keep-this-girl-in-her-place scheme. Taking a slug of his brandy, he retreated and said, "All right, Mr. McCutchan it is."

All through my married life, no matter how awkward or inappropriate it sometimes was, I never broke that rule. I kept it until the day they died. That night when I got in bed, my thoughts kept my emotions in a spinning frenzy. Happiness showed up when I looked at my ring. Excitement (or maybe greed) beamed with hope of a secure financial future. Dread popped in: will I be a McCutchan or not? Fear roared with insecurity: maybe I'm not good enough.

I longed for a good night's sleep, but a new day doesn't change things when you're living in limbo.

Chapter 14:

Social Graces

Life took my roommates and me down different roads, which meant another move. I landed in a new two-floor apartment in the same neighborhood as our rental house. Light streamed in the apartment windows and my indoor plants thrived. My new place, like a feature in *House Beautiful*, matched my furniture perfectly. I loved the neutral colors of the newly painted creamy white walls and the low-pile tan carpet. My upstairs bedroom, complete with my Dutch girl quilt and walk-out balcony, gave me satisfaction and peace. But that peace soon escaped.

Not long after I moved in, I was awakened in the middle of the night by someone or something banging loudly on my front door. I chose to pretend no one was home. Too afraid to go downstairs to see what was going on, I shot up long enough to lock my bedroom door. Then I wrapped my quilt tight around me like a security blanket and, after an eternity, I fell back to sleep.

In the morning, I slowly walked down the stairs, scanning the living room and checking the door. The dead bolt and chain link lock had held. I gingerly opened the door. Woodchips lay in a heap both inside and outside of the doorway. The fractured doorframe, split top to bottom, looked like someone had taken a battering ram to it. Fear reared up within me, and my hands began to shake. I called Bill, my landlord, and the police.

Bill said, "That does it. After we're married you are moving in with me. This place is full of lowlifes."

I wanted so badly to say, "That's what you think I am? I live here. I love living here." But I kept quiet.

Two policemen arrived in response to my call. One took pictures and one completed a thorough interview with intense concern. Police officers and nurses view each other with great mutual respect. The police officer threw out a multitude of questions. I tossed back answers so fast he had to be using shorthand to write it all down.

"Sir, it was 1:00 a.m. when I first heard the banging...No sir, I don't have any enemies that I am aware of...No, I haven't received any threats or phone calls...No, nothing is missing, and I can't imagine anyone wanting to harm me." When all the facts were reviewed the officer presented the following hypothetical conclusion: because all apartments look the same, a drunk may have mistaken my apartment for his own, and when his key didn't work, he got pissed. Regardless of whether it was a drunk, a thief, or a devil, I lied when I said nothing was missing. Whoever it was had stolen my peace of mind.

The landlord immediately got the maintenance crew to work while Bill and I went upstairs to check the bedroom lock and the balcony door. After flipping both locks fifty times each, he finally sat down on my bed. He grabbed the foot-tall flashlight that Grandpa gave me, which I kept on the floor by the nightstand. Whipping the wide headed metal flashlight in the air like a weapon, he said, "Guess you could smack an intruder with this and do some damage."

Clicking the on and off button while peering into the reflector, he shook it, unscrewed it, and dumped six corroded D-cell batteries along with rusty acid onto my quilt. He glared at the batteries and then me. "Donna, didn't you ever think to check the batteries? What good is a flashlight if it doesn't light? Look at the mess you made." I grabbed my quilt off my bed and headed to the sink. But battery acid does more than stain, it eats fabric. All my fault. My stupidity and lack of flashlight maintenance had ruined an irreplaceable treasure—my high school graduation quilt Gram made for me.

My losses were piled high for me in that moment, but like Scarlet O'Hara, I had to think about this another day. This was my day off, and once my apartment was secure, I had to find a wedding dress. I milled through every bridal department in the mall, plucking hangers off the rack, twirling dress after dress, examining price tags, gasping, and quickly returning the beautifully designed masterpieces back in the spaces where they belonged.

Tired of looking, I had decided to give it up for the day when something caught my eye: a long-sleeved ivory top with covered buttons and a matching eyelet skirt with a two-inch silky ribbon belt. I tried it on. Perfect fit! I rushed to the register to make it my own.

The woman at the register said, "This is such a pretty outfit" as she fiddled to find the price tag.

My face felt hot. "Oh, thank you," I said. "It's my wedding dress."

She stopped, took off her glasses, and stared at me for a moment. Then she said, "In that case it's fifty percent off today. Every bride deserves a break." Overwhelmed by the stranger's kindness, I wrote the check, careful not to drip my tears on it, and thanked her.

Weeks before the wedding, the McCutchans' next-door neighbors hosted an engagement party for us at the Country Club. I grew to know the Country Club staff well. Many had worked private parties at the McCutchan house for years. When Mr. and Mrs. McCutchan, Sam and Jane Orr, and Bill and I arrived, we received royal treatment. Gingerly walking between packed tables of physicians, lawyers, and executives and their families, we made our way to the reserved round table by the windows overlooking the golf course.

Bill asked Jane, "What's for supper?"

"I preplanned our meal," she replied. "The main course will be Duck à l' Orange."

Bill blurted, "Oh, I hate duck. I want to order off the menu." Flustered, Jane waved to Mr. George, our waiter, dressed in a crisp white and black uniform. Whispering, she asked "Please bring a menu for Bill." Then Mrs. McCutchan tossed me into the mess using a genuine lie: "Oh Jane, duck is Donna's favorite."

Smiling like a good decoy, I nodded while riding the wave of embarrassment alongside Mrs. McCutchan. After perusing the menu for a few minutes, Bill ordered a cheeseburger and french fries. Sitting back in my chair, amazed at these events, the familiarity of the situation triggered an old memory.

During my senior year in high school, I worked in the kitchen of the Pennsylvania country club. Janet and Pete did the cooking and two of us waitresses took orders, served meals, and cleared tables. We loved working men's night. Men filled with good food and drink sparked lighthearted jovial conversation, generous tipping, and appreciation from everyone except Dr. G. Whenever he finished eating, he stacked all the dirty dishes on the floor beside his feet. The waitress assigned to that table had to lay the brown, round bussing tray on the floor and get on her hands and knees to pick up his mess. Lifting the loaded tray was always the biggest struggle of the night. We loathed that man, devoid as he was of social graces.

Strange how twisted life can be. Now I was sitting with millionaires at the Country Club beside the one lacking social grace and etiquette—my own fiancé.

I soon learned that disrespect and embarrassment can cloth a person in awkwardness whether dished out in public or private. One evening during wedding planning, Mrs. McCutchan said, "Donna, I have something for you. Come with me." I felt funny walking through her bedroom to the most amazing dressing area. It had creamy yellow wooden closets, shelves, and drawers from ceiling to floor. There was enough wardrobe space for four people. She motioned for me to sit on the padded window seat while she produced a shopping bag.

Sharing an intimate moment of transparency, she said, "Over the years I have had multiple cysts removed from my breasts. No one could possibly know because I wear these..." And she pulled out three new padded underwire bras—one white, one taupe, and one black. Continuing her objective, she nonchalantly added "I do believe these will fit you fine," putting them back in the sack. "The men don't need to know about this. Why don't you take them out to the car now so you won't forget them?"

Trying hard to be tactful, I asked, "Mrs. McCutchan how much do I owe you?"

"Oh, never mind that," she replied. "Think of this as an early wedding present." I've never been to a wedding where bras were gifted, especially from a future mother-in-law! Carrying my new McCutchan-approved bras to the car, I wanted to scream, "What, even my boobs aren't big enough to suit you? Too bad you never met my Gram. She wore a 44, but I am sure you could find fault. You'd probably give her the phone number for a plastic surgeon for a reduction."

Slowly walking back from the car, I took a deep breath before opening the huge wooden front door of the mansion. My emotions swirled. Maybe Mrs. McCutchan genuinely wanted me to look good in my clothes. Maybe a 34B is more socially acceptable than a 32A. A big cup is more appropriate, regardless of filling capacity. It seemed like deception to me. This whole scenario reminded me of a joke Gram used to tell:

After a date, this couple kissed goodnight at the girl's front door. When the young man turned to leave the girl said, "Wait a minute, I have something for you." Reaching into her bra she pulled out two orange nerf balls and placed them in his hands. "Here you go! You've been playing with these all night long. You might as well take them with you."

Planning for the wedding meant spending lots of time with Bill's parents. Mrs. McCutchan was a marvelous cook, and I loved everything she served. But I never felt comfortable in that house, especially in the bathroom. Everything sported monograms. A little basket with starched linen cloths sat perfectly stacked to display "CMcC" for "Carol McCutchan." When I washed my hands, I thought about using one of those fancy towels to dry them, but I didn't know the proper place to put a crumpled and dirty used towel. Instead, I dried my hands with toilet tissue as best I could and flushed the evidence.

I confess I also had a problem with the tan bathroom trash basket. I wondered if the basket might be an heirloom of some sort, for it was always empty. I never threw anything in there. I shared this peculiarity with Betty, the McCutchans' housekeeper, who became my friend. She told me, "I'm the same or maybe worse. I push lint balls and tiny pieces of junk paper into my jean pockets when I clean. I empty my pockets in my trash at home, but never here."

If I were a trash basket, I'd love to be full and overflowing. I prefer purpose and functionality over emptiness any day.

Chapter 15:

Where is the Love?

Weddings, no matter how big or small, usually require planning, decision making, and collaboration between the bride-to-be and husband-to-be. Not in my world. Mrs. Mac (the pet name I gave Bill's mother in the privacy of my thoughts) loved planning and knew social mores, so I gladly gave her the reins. Far be it from me to be a source of embarrassment!

Making every effort to please everyone, she tailored our wedding and celebration party like scenes from *Downton Abbey*. The actual wedding ceremony and vows included the common folk and servant types—my nurse friends were generously invited alongside the closest members of the McCutchan clan and a few neighbors. The second act to this grand performance was a huge Country Club marriage celebration party planned for after the honeymoon. Everything came together with McCutchan precision.

We got married in the landmark Johnston Chapel in McCutchan-ville. Bill walked me down the aisle. No one came to give me away; this was not the McCutchans' choice, but mine. Like a lost piece longing to be picked up off the floor and snapped into the McCutchan family portrait puzzle, I did the unthinkable. I did not invite my family to the wedding.

Our wedding day was blessed with blue skies and seventy-degree weather, perfect for the reception party on the mansion's brick terrace, surrounded by blooming dogwoods and mature trees. Before dusk, Bill and I said our goodbyes and started the trip to our honeymoon destination on Kiawah Island, South Carolina. After driving four hours of the eleven-hour trip, Bill pulled into a Best Western in Tennessee and said, "I'm getting sleepy. We're stopping for the night."

I agreed. "Great idea. It's been a long day and I'm tired too."

After check-in, we parked, unloaded the suitcases, and hiked up the back stairs to a room with two queen beds. Bill situated his toiletry bag by the sink as I opened my suitcase to take out my new pink nightgown.

"I'm taking the bed by the bathroom," Bill said, "in case I have to get up in the night."

I stood speechless for a moment, not sure how to respond. Then I washed my face, brushed my teeth, put on my nightgown, and went to bed—in the one closest to the door.

The next day we arrived in Kiawah and settled into our suite. A huge basket with fruits and nuts and bottle of champagne sporting a large purple bow with "Congratulations" printed in silver, sparkly words sat on the dinette table. I felt so blessed to be surrounded by such warmth and beauty. Finally, a happy chapter in the book of my life—a honeymoon beyond comprehension! I thought I had married a true gentleman, one who waited for me to enjoy marital union.

Sex can definitely be awkward, but on a honeymoon one word should be stricken from any conversation. Bill said, "Donna, you're frigid, and I know exactly what to do about this."

The next night after supper, Bill took me to a drive-in movie. At first, I thought, okay, a romantic comedy or love story might be enjoyable. But when I saw the titles on the screen, I cringed.

Bill's eyes gleamed with evil excitement when he explained, "I'd never do this at home. Someone might see me. But no one knows me here."

"I know who you are. I know you. Or maybe I don't know you at all." Disgusting X-rated sex scenes gave whole new meaning to the word honeymoon. Freckles or birthmarks on butts or private parts had to be the only possible way to identify the actors or actresses. After about five minutes of such I leaned my seat back, turned onto my left side, made a pillow roll out of my jacket, curled my legs up on the seat and looked at Bill. His eyeballs, fixed on the screen, reminded me of a bullfrog. The man overflowed with giddy laughter like a child out of parental view for the first time eating all the Easter candy and blaming it on the dog.

I knew the stories of his childhood, the true ones. When he was in kindergarten, he got into the maintenance man's tools and began hammering and redesigning the classroom. What was Mrs. Mac's response to this behavior? She went to kindergarten with him every day, until the teacher banished them both. In middle school, he sent out birthday invitations to a gob of classmates. Children arrived at his house with presents, expecting a party. Mrs. Mac had no idea. It wasn't his birthday.

This kid, this man, my new husband, was gawking at something unacceptable and deplorable, and it exhilarated him more than my nakedness ever could.

I said, "Mac, I'm gonna go to sleep. Please turn the heavy panting down. Off is better."

Mr. McCutchan had given us money for the honeymoon, or I should say he had given Bill money. I never knew how much. My banker husband hated spending money for every meal and decided we would eat out for suppers only. Every bride loves the trip to the grocery store and the daily excitement of preparing breakfast and lunch for her very picky eater of a husband. Of course, doing dishes and cleaning the kitchen gives a woman such pleasure, especially Mrs. Frigid. How could it not?

We took several day trips on our honeymoon journey, and Bill drove me to places his father loved. Stories of the history of the McCutchans, especially his father's life, consumed him.

The day before we went home was the best day of the whole trip. Bill scheduled a fishing expedition with other tourists. I caught a trigger fish, a red snapper, and a sea bass. Each time my pole bent, I'd scream, "I caught one," and a tall, muscular worker in a tank top would carefully walk ledges to get to me. He would then position himself behind me and help reel in my fish, three times. After my first catch, Bill leaned over and whispered in my ear, "Next time you hook one, hand me your rod and let me reel it in." I didn't. I loved that day, and when we got off the boat, the workers told us they could deliver the snapper and sea bass to the restaurant, and we could eat our fish for supper. A triggerfish is a bear to clean, so they tossed it. We went back to our suite, showered, changed, and walked down the lane to the restaurant to enjoy our fish. It was a perfect day for me, and a jealous day for Bill.

Learning each other's idiosyncrasies takes time. I felt it was strange behavior to take a Bible into the bathroom and lock out your bride and have devotions in the throne room. I began to wonder who—or what—I had married.

After our honeymoon trip, the McCutchans threw us a huge marriage celebration party at the Country Club. They invited all their friends. I had never met so many people in one night in my life. Mrs. McCutchan stood by my side, making introductions and conversation.

Surrounded by beautiful people, delicious food, and music, I looked around and felt accepted and honored. Mr. and Mrs. McCutchan genuinely looked happy. Relaxed and content, I let myself believe this future life to be drastically better than my past. That feeling of belonging only lasted until the next day when we opened our gifts, and I received a clear message to the contrary.

Thinking the beautiful silver-embossed paper held a wonderful cookbook, I got a true taste of mother-in-law gall when I pulled the wrapping away to reveal Emily Post's *Etiquette*—the coveted gift every new bride hopes to receive. It was presumably the gift my millionaire mother-in-law hoped would replace my Bible. It didn't.

It was the only virgin book I've ever owned.

Chapter 16:

My Marriage Mirage

The early years of any marriage can be classified in polite terms as an adjustment period. I prefer to shed the façade and admit my marriage was an illusion filled with false hope. Not a lot of tenderness or sensitive loving phrases could be found by rewinding the recordings in my mind. We were crammed into a worn two-bedroom apartment, complete with ugly crap green shag carpet and a kitchen so small I felt like the filling of an Oreo cookie. In that uncomfortable place, Bill—my self-appointed food critic who would rather complain than help—piled on the unkind daily reviews and devalued one of my greatest strengths—cooking.

Wrinkling up his nose, he'd take one bite of my baked chicken, or my stuffed pork chops, or my melt-in-your-mouth pot roast, and then he'd throw down his fork declaring, "Pennsylvania Wet Style. That's the only way you know how to cook. I'd rather eat beef jerky or saltines and sardines." And he did.

Mrs. McCutchan, his mother, knew. A month after the wedding, she presented me with a two-ring binder of index cards with typed recipes, including step-by-step instructions. A stamped label on the little gold binder read, "His favorite things." Chili, spaghetti, pork tenderloin, pecan dreams, and hot bacon coleslaw, to name a few, became acceptable, edible, meals. I thanked Mrs. Mac for the tasteful book.

Within the first few weeks of our married life, Bill informed me of the equal distribution of the household bills. The rent, he paid, a choice justified because his name was on the lease. My responsibilities included the groceries, electricity, and water. Car insurance, car payments, or gas remained the same. Those expenses belonged to us individually and marriage did not change that.

One night, Bill called me into his home office to discuss our marital banking policies. He put a whole new spin on the concept of personal banking. Sitting behind his desk in his leather rolling chair, he explained the need to keep all banking, checking, and saving accounts separate. His rationale was that "more couples divorce over money than anything else. I know this because I am a banker and I see into other people's lives. Some of the physicians you know make over $350,000 and struggle to keep from bankruptcy. High-maintenance wives and especially ex-wives deplete accounts faster than anything. Divorce is dreadful."

After this talk, I found a bit of peace in a twisted commonality between us. I never wanted a divorce because I knew the pain of loss. He never wanted a divorce for fear of loss—financial, of course. We had different reasons, but we shared the same resolve.

I took a Pollyanna approach to this announcement and realized that I had been given a terrific opportunity to save. I didn't have to pay all the bills. This arrangement gave me the opportunity to save and control my money, as I've always enjoyed. I knew before I married Bill that privacy, locked closets, and desk drawers were to be respected. Respect comes easy when you don't have a key. Bill's choice not to share income or banking information with me felt like he had locked me out of that file, too.

The advantage of an August wedding is how fast and full fall and winter fly. By early spring of 1985, we left apartment life. We rented a house on Kratzville Road from Audrey and Jimmie Wallace, friends of Bill's parents. It was a cottage-style house with flowering trees, a lovely yard, big windows, large rooms, a sunroom with louvered windows, and a huge basement for my sewing room. We loved this house.

Bill traveled a lot during this time. His coworkers called him Mac, and I started to as well. Banking regulations were changing, and in 1983 Old National Bank became a multi-bank holding company. Mac and his co-workers in the loan department traveled through the week to sift through loans made by smaller banks prior to their acquisition by Old National. This group of lending officers became close, and Mac loved to razz them, play jokes on them, and embarrass them. Peer retaliation was sweet. One memorable example: small towns rarely support high-end hotels, and one night after a long day's work, Bill pulled back the bedspread and sheets to find piles of mouse turds on his pillow. Of course, the next morning he reported this to the group still working in the Evansville office. Days later, when he finally returned to his desk, piles of chocolate sprinkles stood on his manila files, desk drawers, and computer station. His peers howled, while Bill scowled.

During one of Bill's trips, I called him with life-altering news. "Okay. Are you ready for the results? The strip turned blue. We're gonna have a baby." He took a long breath before he spoke. "Whew, this is a lot to take in. You do know I want a boy."

"Well, I want a healthy baby, and we will love him or her no matter what. And by the way, twins run in my family. Grandpa's sisters, Mae and Della, are identical red-headed twins." Mac hated red heads.

I so enjoyed being pregnant. I enrolled in pregnancy aerobic classes, read excellent books, and kept running down the halls of the Baptist hospital as an IV therapy nurse. My work family and patients have consistently put positive deposits into my emotional bank account all my life. Up at 4:30 a.m., I showered, dressed, enjoyed my breakfast, and arrived at work long before morning sickness saw a ray of daylight. Peers at the hospital joked with me. "You don't get maternity leave. Just deliver that baby, grab up your IV bucket and get back to work."

One morning at work, I had to start an IV on a gentleman needing antibiotics when I was about four to five months along. "Mr. G.," I said, smiling at the dark-eyed 60-year-old patient with his disheveled greasy hair and scraggly beard, "do you mind putting out your cigarette? Smoking makes me nauseated, and I need to start your IV."

"You rotten witch…" and the filthy words flowed.

I calmly raised my hand like a gentle stop sign. "Sir, please watch your tongue. I'm pregnant and my baby can hear every word you're saying." I quickly started his IV and reached back for more tape from the bucket sitting on the bedside table behind me while supporting his arm against my belly. I jumped when he shrieked. "Oh my, Oh my. I just felt that baby kick. Wow, I've never felt a baby kick before." And he began to shout it to other staff, to his roommate, and to anyone else in earshot. "Hey, listen up! I just felt a baby kick!"

His face warmed. His eyes brightened with wonder, and the biggest smile replaced the snarl. I patted his arm and leaned close. "Curse at momma and the baby will kick you every time." He couldn't stop laughing.

That night I told Mac how our baby transformed a grouch. He wasn't impressed. After supper, we watched the news in the living room and the baby kicked again. Excited, I grabbed his hand and placed it on my belly. "Great, you get to feel our baby kicking." He jerked his hand away as if he'd been made to touch a hot stove and said, "I'll play with him when he comes out." What? Like I'm a leper or a surrogate? A cussing stranger got a kick out of a kick, but not my husband. I got the message. The baby is touchable, but not me.

More evidence of his feelings, or lack thereof, came at Christmas. The Old National Bank Christmas party of 1985 made the list of our most embarrassing marriage moments. I think the party was held on an upper floor of the bank building. I do remember the decorations glimmered while the gracious servers scurried to deliver steaming plates of mixed vegetables, roasted potatoes, and prime rib. I pulled my wheat roll apart and reached for the butter when Mac speared my prime rib and slapped it on his plate. He then replaced mine with his. "Mine is nothing but gristle." His peers looked on in disbelief. So did I.

Why I kept clinging to the illusion of a real loving marriage eludes me. Mac's actions kept screaming, "Never gonna happen." I guess hope kept me from hearing the truth. If an unborn baby could change a grouch, could a newborn change Mac?

Chapter 17:

A Time to be Born

C lose to midnight on January 11, 1986, I shook Bill awake. "Mac, get up my water broke. It's time to go to the hospital." He jumped out from under the covers and yelled, "Take these sheets down in the basement and put them in the washer. Make me a cheese and bologna sandwich with mustard and an apple, I might get hungry. Don't forget the napkins and bottled Perrier water. I'm going to shave and wash up."

Like a fool, I stripped the bed linens, held tight to the metal railing for balance, and using great caution descended the steep, narrow basement steps. I ignored Lamaze training that said when a pregnant woman's water breaks, she should get to the hospital as soon as possible. Packing lunches, waddling up and down basement stairs, and doing laundry is not in the manual.

"Hee-hee haw-haw, hee-hee haw-haw." Stopping twice to breathe through contractions during the climb back to the kitchen, I jammed his lunch order into a brown sack and screamed, "We need to leave right now! Mac come on. We need to go. Contractions are coming fast."

Mac grabbed the hospital bag by the kitchen door that I packed weeks ago. Finally, we were out the door. Mac popped open the hatchback of his white Toyota Supra and tossed the purple American Tourister satchel in the back. Just as I opened my door, Mac jumped in front of me. His arm shot up like a gate in front of a parking garage, blocking me from entrance.

In a threatening tone he warned, "Don't sit down yet. Don't you dare sit down. I'll be right back." He scrambled into the house and soon returned with six folded multi-colored beach towels. "Can't have you ruin my red leather seats." I felt like a cross between a beached whale, a leaky faucet, and a giraffe in a tiny box. I said, "Mac, maybe you should open the moon roof. If you hit a bump you will break my neck."

Screeching up to the ER doors, Mac put the car in park and ran inside to get help. A pleasant transport person helped me into a wheelchair and whooshed me to labor and delivery. In my room, I shed my clothes and donned a hospital gown. My labor and delivery nurse, Meghan, introduced herself. Her sweet, giddy demeanor was enjoyable as she ran through the script of admission questions. During the familiar questions and answers, I let her know I was a nurse.

In between taking my temperature and blood pressure, she asked "Where do you work?"

"I've been a nurse since 1978. I work at the Baptist hospital. By the way, I need the bedpan."

At this point, Mac walked into the room. He had parked the car and completed the required insurance forms, and once he arrived, he took a seat on the couch near the window. He nervously fidgeted with a legal pad organizer and pen.

"Meghan," I repeated, "I need the bedpan. I know since my water broke, I can't get out of bed to go to the bathroom, so please bring me a bedpan."

A stern look came over Meghan's cheerful face. "Oh, no. You can't have a bedpan. You're a Prim-ip. I mean this is your first baby and it is the pressure of the baby's head you feel. You just think you have to go to the bathroom."

I glared at her while I blew through contractions, clutched the sheet in my fists and blasted Meghan. "I have been with my body longer than you. I'm going to have diarrhea. Get me a bedpan. Now."

Shaking her head emphatically, she stammered, "Okay, but first, I have to check to see how far dilated you are."

"Look, I know protocol. But Sister, I'm telling you now if you put your hand down there you're gonna be sorry. Get me a bedpan."

And she obliged. She threw a shiny, silver pan on my bed and disappeared. I never thought a bedpan could look so good. Relief at last! I filled it twice. And Mac emptied it both times. Standing in the doorway of the bathroom, clean bedpan in hand, straight-faced Bill said, "I knew when you came in here you were gonna make a big stink, but I had no idea it was gonna be this bad."

My "hee-hee haw-haw" danced on waves of laughter.

Nurse Meghan came back, and I apologized for my behavior. "My husband can testify to the fact there was no baby in the bedpan." All was forgiven.

The night dragged, and so did my progress. Mac sat in the corner, chomped on his bologna and cheese sandwich, and sipped Perrier. Mac seemed fixated on the contraction recorder. Looking at the monitor, he kept scribbling on the legal pad on his lap. "Hey, Donna, you will never believe how fast these contractions are coming. Do you want me to tell you?"

"Really, Mac? You think I don't know. Just shut up and leave me alone."

By morning a Pitocin drip was added to my IV to strengthen contractions and help move labor along, but the baby did not like the drip. With each enhanced contraction his heart rate fell from 160 to 80 beats per minute. They rolled me into the surgical suite for a C-section.

On January 12, 1986 at 9:10 a.m., William Alexander McCutchan came into the world, weighing five pounds, eight and a half ounces and measuring eighteen and three-quarter inches long. William spent one day in the special care nursery because the umbilical cord had been wrapped around his neck twice. I thanked the Lord that William was healthy.

Mac went home to have a drink with his father to celebrate the birth of his son. "I have to get some sleep. I've been up all night. I'm exhausted. See you later." As usual, Mac mattered most to Mac. He came the next morning before going out of town for work. Holding William, who was swaddled and sleeping, Mac kept stroking his tiny head and gazing as if in a trance. He couldn't take his eyes off his son, nor his critical eyes off me.

"Get up and get your makeup on. Curl your hair. You look terrible."

I got up every morning and did exactly as he demanded, but for whom? Mac couldn't see me from the bank in southern Indiana, Illinois, Kentucky, or wherever he happened to be working. I spent my hospital time alone with my newborn. I rocked, held, sang to, loved, and snuggled my little darling every day of my hospitalization. My only concern had nothing to do with Mac. I was worried because William never cried. I got permission to give him a bath and still, he never shed a tear. That didn't seem natural.

On the day of our discharge, Mac never came to the hospital to bring William and me home. Instead, he went to work, in town, in the Evansville office. He chose work. He had plenty of personal time and family medical leave. Work trumped caring for his own family. Truth is, I felt the need to climb the ladder of success meant more to Mac than I did.

Heap feelings of imposition onto feelings of rejection and the heaviness is unbearable. I felt so bad. Mac imposed upon his mother. She loaded up her car with a baby seat, her 84-year-old husband, and coolers filled with gourmet foods, salads, and nutritional drinks. Then she picked up her son's family from the hospital and brought us home to Kratzville Road, which had to sting. When my delivery date drew near Mrs. McCutchan had invited us to stay with them in their home with the baby. I had refused as politely as possible. I said, "No. Thanks, but no.

William's nursery was stocked with a new couch, a changing table, and Mac's crib with the eyelet crib skirt and big full bumper pads that I made myself. Two huge bunnies hung on the wall above his bed. I had sewn kimonos and bibs. Everything was ready for baby's homecoming. My C-section saved William's life and helped ease tension between me and my mother-in-law. Mrs. McCutchan's guest bedrooms and nursery were upstairs and after my emergency C-section, the stairs were out of the question.

We got home around lunchtime, and I was unable to help Mrs. McCutchan carry things into the house. I hated to see her struggling with coolers and sacks of groceries. My surgery put me on a lift restriction. About an hour after we settled in, Mac waltzed through the door. Peer pressure had propelled him home. Laughing, he told us what had happened.

His loan review officemates had surrounded his desk. Rodney asked, "Aren't Donna and little William coming home from the hospital today?"

"Yep. Mom and Dad are taking them home."

"What on earth are you doing here? Go home. What is wrong with you?"

Mac thought that was hilarious. I thought it was heartless and wanted to cry.

After a few days at home William finally cried. For seven weeks of my eight-week maternity leave, he cried every day and I thought he'd never stop. Hello, colic!

Chapter 18:

My Scarlet Letter is "D"

otherhood is exhausting, especially when the newborn cries with colic all day long. Of course, Mac's father blamed it on my breast milk. As the CEO of Mead Johnson, one the largest makers of infant formula in the United States, he believed human milk was inferior despite research touting its contributions to immunity and its built-in vitamins and nutrients. I didn't care what the millionaires thought.

I loved getting up at 4:00 a.m. to feed my baby—something only I could do. A blanket of peace covered little William and me as we rocked and held onto each other in the nursery. No one disturbed our sacred moments of serenity. No negative thoughts, critical tongues, or feelings of insecurity ever entered the nursery at that hour. Then, morning came.

During the day, Mrs. McCutchan came over with a cooler of salads, gourmet meats, fruits, and protein shakes. And, of course, special hamburgers, Tater Tots, and childish foods for her fussy, spoiled baby boy Bill.

Because the cause of colic is unknown, no medication was available to relieve William's symptoms. He arched his back, drew up his tiny legs, and cried in anguish as belly cramps, gas, and explosive diarrhea continued. Mrs. McCutchan, Bill, and I took turns trying calming methods.

Finally, when William was eight weeks old, I called the pediatrician's office in a panic.

"I need your help. My baby has been sleeping for an hour. His skin is warm and dry, respirations are thirty."

"Mrs. McCutchan, how old is your baby?" asked the nurse who answered my call.

"Eight-weeks today."

"Oh, I see. This is called a nap and he should be doing this several times during the day for an hour or two. This is normal."

Feeling condescending platitudes flowing into my fatigued, foggy brain, I attempted to change the nurse's perception of my idiocy.

"But you don't understand, since we brought him home from the hospital he has never slept during the day. I sighed. He has colic."

Like an angel from heaven the nurse softened her tone and whispered, "He had colic yesterday, but not today, and most likely not tomorrow. Once it's gone, it won't be back." And she was right.

Life got better. We found a lovely babysitter and I returned to work. For the next few months, William thrived on a routine complete with scheduled naptime and bedtime. He slept all through the night and rarely cried; I cried, often, with joy.

Mrs. McCutchan loved to get her hands on her grandson, whom she referred to as Master William. She paid for me to have tennis lessons at the country club. During my lessons, she volunteered to watch William. Learning backhand, forehand, and serving moves came easy for me. The old ballerina, tap dancer, fire baton twirler, and cheerleader in me loved to learn a new sport, and at twenty-nine, I relished the thought of dropping the twenty-two unwanted pregnancy pounds. I agreed to the setup, until the day Mrs. McCutchan unabashedly labeled me an underling.

I couldn't wait to tell my husband about the offense. Mac had stopped by to grab a drink with his father, a normal occurrence for those two. When he walked through the kitchen door around 6 p.m., I doubt he knew a wife could come to a rolling boil quickly when a mother-in-law is the heat source.

Sitting in a table chair with a billed cap on his head, William kicked his feet and reached for his daddy with his little fists opening and closing, signaling "Pick me up, Pick me up!" Hs father obliged.

I asked Bill, "How was your day?"

Raising his eyebrows and crinkling up his nose while he winked and smiled at William, he said, "Had to review some loans that I know we will have to call in. Tomorrow I'll pull a prominent person's credit cards and they'll probably have to sell the grand piano that pushed them over the edge. How was your day?"

"William and I had a great day, until this afternoon when your mother stopped by." I stopped cleaning strawberries and took a drink of ice water from my big Styrofoam cup. "Your mother brought over a sack of tennis clothes for me. Let me show you."

Walking over to the kitchen table, I held up the aqua- and white-striped top and pointed to the huge orange-brown stain under the collar. Then I showed him the rest. "Mac, just look at this pair of shorts. The entire crotch is ripped apart." I peered at him through the crotch then stuck my arm through the hole. Picking up the faded pink tennis skirt, I turned it inside out to showcase the partially unattached and frayed hand-hemming attempt that someone had made.

Mac's mom may have thought she served this set with advantage as a winner, but I made the decision to chip, charge, and chop. As usual Mac said nothing. "Well, I called your mother and asked, 'Did you want these clothes returned after my lessons are over?' And you won't believe what she said to me…"

"What?" Mac said, smiling and concentrating more on Master William's attempt to remove his ruby tie pin than our conversation.

"She said, 'Heavens no, if I wanted those clothes back, I would never have given them to you in the first place.' Can you believe how cruel? She signs me up for tennis lessons, then gives me disgusting tennis outfits not fit for wear."

"I'm sure she didn't mean anything by this."

I lost control. My Styrofoam cup of ice water became a Mac-seeking missile that missed his head by an inch and exploded onto the kitchen wall. Mac's mouth hung gaping. He grabbed a dish towel, put Master William into his table seat, and sopped up the slippery icy water puddle.

"Mac, I am done. I've had enough. I want a divorce."

Game, set, match.

Chapter 19:

Clandestine Counseling

M ac tried his best to save himself from the embarrassing stigma of divorce, so he agreed to counseling. There was one stipulation: he got to choose the counselor. At this point, I simply didn't care.

He settled on a man—a Baptist minister—from another town and scheduled late-night sessions for us. He was paranoid about the possibility that someone might find out, and it caused him no end of stress. Imagine a banker in a suit and tie sneaking up the back stairs to attend private marriage counseling to appease his broken-hearted wife. Truly, a shameful experience!

Mixed feelings of fear and uncertainty kept bouncing about in my gut. I guess I had never expected Mac to agree to counseling, and I worried I'd be the one sacrificed on the altar of blame. I imagined the Baptist preacher's mini sermons directed to me alone, exploring topics like "divorce is not an option," "submit to your husband" and "repent and pray more." My negative thinking and critical self-talk made me nervous. Mac also looked pale and uncomfortable as he frowned at me and then rang the minister's doorbell.

To our surprise, the door opened and a 6-foot-5, 200-plus-pound man with a warm smile greeted us at the door. "You must be the McCutchans." He encouraged us to come in with a gentle sweep of his right arm. "Please take a seat and make yourselves at home. Can I get you two a pop or water?" This was our first introduction to Freddie.

"Water would be nice," I said, and Mac nodded "yes" to Freddie as well.

We sat in overstuffed chairs in a circle. Freddie looked so different from the picture I had conjured up. His thick salt and pepper hair parted perfectly to the right. Large dark rimmed glasses framed his dancing gray-blue eyes. His easy smile and nonverbal demeanor exuded an immediate message: "You can trust me."

Our initial session began with a getting-to-know-you survey. Freddie shared a snapshot of his personal and professional background, probably as an example to put us at ease. Then, using a similar pattern of discovery, he gently unraveled the differences between Mac and me. A wise counselor, he took us back to the beginning—our childhoods. We took turns talking without interrupting each other. Very seldom did Freddie take notes. I don't believe anyone ever listened to me or looked at me so intensely. All our nervousness vanished.

Knowing a client's backstory is important to counselors. Discussions of our childhood family dynamics helped highlight similarities and differences between us. Mac and I came from two different family systems, and as our weekly counseling sessions continued, I saw things about Mac in a new light. Mac's childhood and adolescence, for example, had escaped the pain of divorce, but he understood death at an earlier age than most people should.

Early in our sessions, Freddie gave Mac an assignment. "Before you leave for work each morning, hold Donna in your arms for two minutes." Imagine Mac in a Brooks Brother's suit, starched striped shirt, and coordinated tie with his right arm like a noose around my neck. His eyes were focused on the second hand of his wristwatch for the entirety of the exercise. When time was up, he released me from the choke hold and said, "Got to get to work. I'll see you tonight." Mac never missed a morning. But he misunderstood the meaning of a word. A choke hold is not synonymous with "hold your wife."

During discussions at Freddie's, we used a white and bright blue toy boat to enhance our listening and communication skills. Whoever held the boat did the talking. Sadly, the bottom of our boat fell out during one intense session.

Freddie asked, "How was your week?"

I took the lead, looking at Freddie. "Not good." I turned to my husband. "Do you agree, Mac?"

He nodded.

Head tilted to one side, Freddie leaned forward. "What happened?"

As Mac sat silent with his head down, I laid down the foundation of the story. Freddie already knew about the tennis clothes fiasco.

"I came home from a tennis lesson and told Mac, I had to quit."

Mac stumbled over his words as he explained. "I told her not to quit. I hated to see her quit. She loved it and she was doing so well and was truly good at it."

Freddie frowned. "Give me the gory details. What could have happened to make you quit, Donna?"

"When I went into the building to sign Mrs. Mac's name for the lesson, the pro pushed me against the wall and kissed me. I pushed him back and reminded him we both were married." I looked at Mac, who stared at the floor. "I knew I my tennis days were over."

"And Mac, how did that make you feel?" Freddie prompted.

As if scrolling through a list of appropriate emotions from the Rolodex in his mind, after what felt like twenty minutes, Mac made a selection. "Anger. That's the feeling," he said, "I was angry."

For the first time, I looked at the man seated beside me and understood the root cause of our pain. I couldn't believe what he was saying because when I had told him about the incident, he just stood in the bedroom dumbfounded. It caused no facial muscle tensions, no grimace, no tears, no remarks, no discussion, just retreat. His response that night was just "I'm going to bed."

Puzzled, I considered several terrible thoughts. Mac can't identify emotions. Maybe he concentrates so hard on giving people the correct answer, he can't select his own. Or perhaps he can't express a feeling. One thing was certain, a disconnect existed. A seed of pity for my husband sprouted that night. I felt sorry for Mac.

In early spring 1986, we completed our therapy sessions. I tried hard to understand and to be more sensitive to a man who suffered from emotional constipation. I threw myself into work, motherhood, and teaching Sunday school.

Confronting the tennis pro or having him terminated never occurred to Mac. Avoiding conflict came more easily for him. He let it go. I didn't. When the pro and I walked to the building to sign for my final lesson, I casually said, "By the way, I told Mac you kissed me."

He stopped in his tracks, his face flushed. "You did what? I could lose this job. I can't believe you did that. I'll get fired."

Satisfaction filled my heart as I witnessed an attack of reality; he was a successful man with a beautiful family and a job at the Country Club that could go away in a kissing minute. Other than my husband, I never told another person, and as far as I knew, neither did Mac. Hopefully, I helped save the tennis pro's marriage, at least.

I began to see no one had a charmed life, not even Mac. I chose to stay, to give us another chance. I kept hoping. Gray skies were sure to clear up, or so I thought. But I was wrong. Blue skies hid behind the black cloak of the death angel who snatched up souls in Pennsylvania.

Chapter 20:

My Favorite

The phone rang one Saturday morning and to my surprise, it was Dad. "Honey, I need a nurse. I've got a pain in my abdomen, and I know there is something wrong."

"Well Daddy," I said, "Go to the doctor."

Hesitation preceded his confession. "I don't have one. All I have is the VA."

"Daddy, you know I worked at Duke and the VA was across the street. I never heard a bad word about the VA. Call and make an appointment. Please keep me in the loop."

And he did. The May spring-cleaning bug bit me hard, but I stopped washing the sunroom windows when I heard the phone again.

"First of all," he said, "I want you to know, I never want to hear the word enema again. Very embarrassing, my butt in the air and a scope to go where no one had ever gone before to find nothing. But...I know something isn't right."

"Okay Dad. Here's what I want you to do. Call your doctor and tell him your daughter is a critical care nurse who has worked at Duke University Medical Center. Tell them to schedule a laparoscopic procedure.

They will make a small incision near your belly button and insert a tube with a tiny camera. If you have a problem, great, the mystery will be solved. If they don't see something suspicious, we will know what we've always known. You're simply crazy."

The procedure solved the mystery and knocked "crazy" off the list of suspects. Colon cancer took its place—the same invader that had stolen the life of Grandma Grace, Dad's mom.

Dad was admitted to the VA hospital in May of 1986. He underwent an open and closed surgery. A tumor the size of a grapefruit was found with metastasis to the liver. Cancer antigen markers were well over 3000. I knew the diagnosis was grave and that he didn't have much time.

I called Mom and Rip, got plane tickets, and took off work so that William and I could go on our first of many airplane adventures.

Flying from Indiana to Pennsylvania with an industrious, five-month-old, purse, and diaper bag, required the center core balance I'd learned from my ballerina days. We settled into our seats and William happily reached for his shoestrings. He slept through most of the three-hour flight.

As we landed and prepared to disembark, a businessman, probably a banker or accountant, dressed like Mac in an expensive charcoal-gray suit, crisp purple and white striped shirt, and purple diamond-patterned tie, stopped by my seat. With concern and sincerity, he offered, "Can I please help carry your bags? You've got quite a precious load."

"I would love the help." And I handed him my diaper bag and tote. I can't thank you enough." He made me wish Mac had cared enough to take off work.

Mom and Rip waited at the gate. They only lived forty-five minutes from the VA hospital and had agreed to help me with William while I visited Dad. We gathered the baggage, tossed it in the truck, and headed home to Boileau Place. I called the VA after supper and the nurse let me know that Dad had a fever of unknown origin. "We're not sure if it is infection or just from his cancer. It's best if you don't come until we know for sure."

Mom put a playpen in the family room. Rip designed a rolling car—a board covered a with a soft rug, four casters, and a rope handle—for William to play with. William laid on his belly and held onto the edges, and we rolled him all over the house. Rip christened William with a nickname: Spud.

William made himself busy, babbling and blowing raspberries the whole time. Despite all the new toys, William also worked feverishly at a new self-imposed challenge. Pulling his left arm out of his teal-blue velour shirt, he laughed as his long sleeve dangled and swung about. I confess improvising and creating new toys out of anything is a talent. I used to put William in a Pampers box and make car noises as I pushed the cardboard car around the living room; this is probably one reason Rip's Spud-mobile was such a hit.

The next morning, a nurse called to give us the all clear. "Blood counts are in and you can bring that baby anytime. No infection!" I called Dad and could hear the excitement in his voice.

"This is great news. I can't wait to see the little fella."

Knowing how important it was to Dad to see his grandson, Mom agreed to go with me to the VA. Dad greeted us with a big smile. "Come on Grandma, sit down beside me so we can have a picture."

It was so unreal, seeing Mom and Dad sharing bed space with my round Gerber baby William sandwiched tightly between them in a red-and-white striped onesie, matching red socks, and soft white shoes. I quickly took several pictures with my cheap camera. Cordial, kind, and awkward, I tried hard to remember the last time I was in the same room with my parents. Nauseating scenes from the courtroom custody battle tried to creep into my head, but I pushed them away as I focused on the picture of today.

I waited a day or two, and when I was certain William was comfortable in his new surroundings, I left him with Mom and Rip to see Dad one more time before I went back home. Then I did something incredibly stupid. I pulled the pack of pictures from my purse and said, "Dad, wait until you see what I've got for you. It's the pictures of you and Mom and William."

His response floored me. "Oh no, do I really look that bad?"

What was I thinking? Cancer isn't pretty. For Dad colon cancer invaded his liver and changed the whites of his eyes and his skin to an unnatural orangish-yellow known as jaundice. I felt as if I had just made Dad the poster child for cancer without his permission. I felt awful.

I spent the entire day with Dad at the VA. Dad spent our time together dwelling on negative past events no one could change. He told me the only reason he married Mom—possible pregnancy. Doing the right thing took moral courage, only to find out she had cysts or something. Then after my brother was born, he listened to a physician's advice, "Keep her pregnant. She's happy when she's pregnant." Then he shared more details than I cared to hear regarding his hatred toward Grandpa and Grandma and Rip. Like a mute with elephant ears, I listened, nodded, and watched a father so full of cancerous hate holding onto haunting memories. I felt sorry for him.

I know death. I'm a nurse. Nurses hear its footsteps, feel its presence, know its ways, and understand its truth. No one escapes the death angel. I knew Daddy would die, and soon, yet somehow life events had murdered him years ago.

Dad shared stories about my childhood. Taking hold of my hand, he whispered, "You were always my favorite." Some words sour a stomach like too many cups of coffee and no food. Me? The one he called a whore? His favorite? Amazing. Daddy didn't remember words I may never forget. But the thought of being a favorite child reminded me of a patient story.

I once walked into a room filled with visitors and asked my patient, "Billy, who are all these people?" Sitting in his recliner, legs propped up with pillows, oxygen flowing through a nasal cannula, he proudly introduced me to every one of his eight siblings. Using his pale, bony pointer, between slow labored breaths he named each one in rank and order. "This is Susie the eldest, then Joey, Sammy, Janie, Scotty, then me, then the dark-haired twins Tina and Tammy, and John is the youngest."

"Wow, I bet you had a wonderful time during the holidays. Did you have great parents?"

Susie said, "We all helped on the farm and Dad rarely had time to do much else, but work. Momma, she was quite the character. Passed away last year and even at her funeral she had us in tears. Not sad tears mind you, but she had us laughin like crazy."

John perked up and chimed in. "I'm the one that started that fire!"

"True as always, baby boy!" jabbed Billy, my patient. Snickers and giggles filled the room. "We were standing around the coffin and Mom was just at peace, dressed in her favorite Sunday pink and blue flowered print dress with the covered buttons and lace bodice. She wore white gloves and a little Bible was propped beside her. John isn't known for tactful conversation or timing, so he blurted out in front of us, 'I hate to tell you all, but you might as well know, I was Momma's favorite.'"

Susie continued, "We all snapped our heads around, smirked, and as if we rehearsed it, in unison we screeched "'What?'"

"Well, it's true," John said. "Momma told me herself several times and made me promise not to tell any of you."

Susy countered, "She told me I was her favorite when we were doing laundry every Monday."

Then Sammy confessed, "Me, too, when it was my turn to help her in the kitchen."

"As we realized what Momma had done, I swear, we could see her laughin in that casket." Smiling at the memory, Billy shook his head.

"She had us in tears all right. The kind of tears she loved us to share. Tickling tears that come from belly laughing so hard your eyes start juicing till they spill over and run down your cheeks. Momma used to warn us that when we get old, laughter can even drip down your leg too. Overflow, ya know?"

I wondered if her headstone is engraved with Momma, Our Favorite. What a lucky family. I bet Dad did the same with Terry, Patti Marie, and me—Dad's favorites.

On the way back to Mom's I drove by the old cement block house on Harmonsburg Road, where a family of five once slept, ate, played, and fought. I drove slowly and cried for many reasons. Dad was going to die. He had dreams and they did not come true. I spent one of our last days together hearing the wrongs people had done to him over the years. His stories broke my heart.

A few minutes later I drove past the old tavern, remembering the day the school bus broke down in two feet of snow and all of us elementary kids had to go inside and wait for a new bus. It was before 7:00 a.m., dark, spooky, and complete with men gathered around the bar and pool table, smoking cigarettes and drinking. It scared me to death. This day, it made me laugh. I never thought an old memory snapshot could overtake my day of sadness. I wiped my face with tissues and resolved, no more crying.

As I pulled into the driveway at Mom's, my head cleared as I thought of hugging William, eating supper, and taking a bath in the cast-iron clawfoot tub. Surely, a good night's sleep could catapult me out of the fuzzy funk I was in. I walked into the kitchen and found Rip lying on the floor playing with my son.

"Where's Mom?"

"Your grandad had another heart attack, so she is on the way to Brookville Hospital."

I knew it was about a two-hour drive, but Mom probably cut off thirty minutes and multiple drivers.

The phone rang. "Go ahead and answer," Rip said, pointing to the phone, "that will be your mom letting us know she got there safe."

"Hello."

An unfamiliar rude voice on the other end of the phone demanded, "Who is this?"

Startled, I said, "This is Donna. Dee's daughter. Who is this?"

"Your grandmother's friend, Jane. Your grandad had a massive heart attack. He's dead."

I went numb. Grandpa dead. My favorite.

Chapter 21

Dead Daze or Awe Struck

Whenever illness and death show up, family members living nearby end up with major responsibilities. Out-of-towners swoop in, skedaddle out, return to work, pretend a smidgen of normalcy still exists, and await the next emergency call. Everyone knows, especially nurses, Death's appetite is like Lay's potato chips—he just can't take one. Usually it's three.

Grandpa got snatched up in early June 1986. Daddy passed weeks later in July. Strange things happened during both deaths.

Mom, Patti, and I stayed at Gram's after Grandpa died. Patti and I sleeping in the same bed, cooking, and doing dishes together in the kitchen felt strange and wonderful. The little white house overflowed with people, but without Grandpa, a sad emptiness hovered over every moment we spent there.

I had never seen Gram in such a bizarre state of mind. She acted like a robotic doll. She slapped on a plastic smile under smeary bright red lipstick. Her great-grandson played on a quilt on the living room floor and she stared at him. William was within her grasp, but she never reached for him. She never held him. Perhaps she was too busy holding in emotions to put on a good front. Then, I figured it out. Gram practiced what she preached. She bucked up.

One summer day when I was fifteen, I watched *Love Story* and openly cried as this woman died of cancer. Gram made fun of me while making lunch. She mocked every sound, every cry, every sob. Then she said, "Buck up. It's just a make-believe movie."

During Grandpa's death and funeral, Gram demonstrated to everyone the way to buck up. There were no tears, no sobs, and no evidence of heartbreak for public or family viewing. Then again, I wasn't with her in the ER. Maybe she fell apart then. Maybe she cried herself to sleep at night. One thing I have learned from years of nursing is that everyone responds differently to death and loss. No one can judge another's behaviors.

One day on the cardiac unit, the wife of a dying man taught me this. The wife explained with confidence and calm, "I know without a doubt Herman will be in heaven. He is such a good man." Then he passed, and before I knew it, the wife's calm did an about face. Grabbing her husband by the shoulders, she began to yell and shake the living tar out of his freshly spirit-fled body. "Get back here Herman, Get back here. This is not the way this should happen. Get back here. You are not to die right now. Get back here!"

I stood in awe. Pure awe.

Gram dealt with Grandpa's death in her own way. Her aloof behavior made me miss Grandpa even more. I could only imagine my little boy in Grandpa's arms in the rocker, sleeping close to his heart. Busting with pride, I just know how it would have been. And I struggled with God. Why did Dad get to see my baby and Grandpa didn't get the chance? That's when the "if onlys" tormented me.

Grandpa had suffered a mild heart attack the weekend before he died. If only I had brought William to Sigel first. If only Gram had called 911. They have oxygen and nitroglycerin on emergency vehicles. If only

Jane hadn't taken over and decided to throw him in the back seat of her car because she could get him to the hospital faster than an ambulance. If only Grandpa had taken his nitro. He hated the headache, so he didn't. "If only" only heaps guilt and blame and multiplies pain. "If only" is powerless to bring those we love back to life.

Growing up, my siblings and I attended multiple funerals. Grandpa lost so many of his brothers and sisters to heart attacks at or before sixty-two. Then he outlived them all. He died in his late seventies. Visitation at the funeral home looked like a celebrity life celebration. I never saw so many grown men cry in my life. Grandpa touched a lot of lives. Men and women from all over came to show respect, tell stories of his generosity, and let tears fall freely.

William and I got back home safe. In a few weeks, I flew back to Pennsylvania again. Cancer took Dad in mid-July. This time, I went alone. William stayed home with Mac and the McCutchans.

I flew into Pennsylvania for Dad's funeral with mixed feelings. I hated to leave my son and go through another funeral, but I also felt guilty. Patti lived in Meadville, and taking care of Dad had fallen to her. Patti, the youngest and wildest of three kids, did that hard job well. When she called me to tell me he died, she said, "I can't wait to see you. I have something to tell you."

When we finally got a moment together, she shared this story. One morning was particularly hard for her so, she put out a distress call to the only help available. She called Mom.

"Mom, can you and Rip please come and help me? I thought I could do this, but I can't. Dad is really, really bad and I have to get him to the VA." Miserable, Dad kept moaning. He was unable to get comfortable in the hospital bed in the living room.

Mom said, "I'll talk to Rip and call you back."

Patti cried, gently patting the limp hand that once loved to tie flies for fishing, plant trees, golf, cook, and hunt. "It's gonna be O.K. Dad.

I'll get you to the hospital. You're gonna be OK." After she bathed and shaved him for the day, Patti got comfortable on the living room floor by his bed and worked a word search puzzle. While he was usually coherent and pleasant, on that day Elmer talked gibberish all day long. Then suddenly, plain as day he asked, "Where did you come from and why are you dressed in all white?"

Startled, Patti raised her head and looked around the room, wondering "Who in the world is he talking to?" She saw no one. His first coherent statement of the day made no sense. "Dad, are you, all right?" she asked. In response, she only got more gibberish.

Less than ten minutes later, the beams of Mom and Rip's headlights came through the window and illuminated the entire living room. Relief and uncertainty arose in Patti's mind. What could possibly happen? Thirty years of mutual hate were about to collide. In one of life's great ironies, Mom and Dad were about to be together in the end as they'd been together in the beginning.

Patti and Mom scurried about to collect toiletries to take with Elmer to the hospital. A problem arose. He needed to be dressed for the trip to the hospital, but weakness made him unsteady and unable to stand. His ex-wife and daughter did not feel comfortable or strong enough to tackle the mission. Dressing duty fell to Rip, the muscle-bound ex-boxer, who Elmer always referred to as the devil who tore apart his family. All his life Elmer vowed to take Rip out by shooting him.

Standing beside the hospital bed in the living room, Rip said, "Elmer, put your hands on my shoulders while I pull up your pants." Dad's skin shone golden orange and yellow, and his belly was swollen from cancer. Rip had to use the last notch of the belt to keep Elmer's pants up.

Face-to-face with Rip, up close and personal for the last time, Elmer said, "Rip, take a good look at me. Do you know where you will be spending eternity? I need you to know I forgive you. I forgive you and Dee both for what you have done to my family."

Rip carried Elmer to the car and Patti Marie took him on his last trip to the VA. Dad died the next night.

Just like all the other out-of-towners we flew in like a flock of homing pigeons. We women sitting in the front row near the grave site shrieked and sobbed when seven soldiers standing behind us fired three shots in unison for the twenty-one-gun salute. The sickening smell of gun powder flooded the air with each eardrum-breaking blast. I wanted those soldiers to stop firing, but when silence fell it was equally unbearable.

Dad had few family members, and Mom and Rip invited them to their Victorian home for a light meal after the funeral. Rip's atheist heart kept replaying the forgiveness scene. As we worked together in the kitchen he kept asking, "Donna, why didn't he shoot me? He threated to shoot me a million times and he was a great shot. Why didn't he have his shotgun loaded? He could have killed me. What would they have given him, life?"

Dad did shoot Rip, after all. God loaded the gun with forgiveness. Dad got life—eternal life in Heaven.

Chapter 22:

The Farm

L oss of a loved one is not like a cold. You don't get over it. You adapt and hang out with this thing called grief, an unpredictable emotional tsunami capable of whipping away any secure hold. That's exactly what happened to me.

I got back to Indiana, my sweet little boy, my banker husband, my church family, and my job. Life's routine, a welcome distraction from grief, helped me smile again. Until the day I ran to a code blue and entered the room of a Grandpa look-a-like. He had the same haircut, the same build, the same rough mechanic hands and muscular forearms, and the same gray look of death. Our efforts were futile. Another life was taken by a massive myocardial infarction.

I didn't want the code team to see me fall apart. I ran down the hall to the staff bathroom, locked the door, sat on the floor and sobbed. I used toilet paper as tissues and noticed my hands shaking uncontrollably. I was a mess.

That night after supper I told Mac. He let me quit work for a while. We had been paying a babysitter handsomely to watch William, and he justified the decision as a money saver.

During the same month, we got a call from a Welborn General surgeon, Dr. Harned. He called to give us the opportunity to purchase his parents' home. A year before I had stopped him in the hall and told him my husband had always admired that property, and if his parents ever thought of selling to let us know. The surgeon remembered, Mac negotiated a price over the phone, and voila, we owned an old home on a five-acre plot in McCutchanville.

Buy a home built in the 1800s as-is and you might as well sing "We've Only Just Begun" with each step you take. Dr. Harned's family claimed a large portion of his parents' remaining belongings, but that still left the closets and barn overflowing. I never saw so many newspapers, magazines, books, clothes, and men's ties. Grandpa used to say, "You don't know how the other half lives and honestly, you don't want to know." Sorting a lifetime of a stranger's stuff is easy. Workers at the Goodwill knew us by name.

When the closet cleanup was done, a new adventure began: remodeling. I confess ignorance of the amount of work this old house needed. I discovered that scheduling painters, plumbers, electricians, stonemasons, carpenters, roofers, hardwood floor finishers, and wallpaper hangers required specific sequencing. Some worked by contract, some by days, and if it was possible to shave off costs, I jumped to help.

I did things I never thought I could. I became an experienced wallpaper stripper, balancing on a ladder while spraying the ceiling with a magical paste-dissolving solution. I probably should have donned a garbage bag or a raincoat and hat, for the blue bandana covering my hair didn't repel the raindrops that kept falling on my head. The baptism of DIF wallpaper remover running down my arms was an unforgettably slimy experience. Twirling a putty knife and scraper to gently peel and pull down heavy canvas-like sheets of dirty cream-colored wallpaper truly is an art. The purpose of wallpapering a ceiling eluded me, until the paper came off and revealed the ceiling cracks it had covered.

After work, Mac came by the farm, inspected progress, put William in his car seat and went home for supper with his parents. Then they went home to our rental house. I often stayed at the farm, working until 10:30 or 11:00 p.m.

Like peeling an onion, every project tackled required the removal of layers and layers of material. Instead of removing the old surface, scrubbing things clean, and installing something new, I learned that previous owners preferred a cover-up process.

The eighth and last layer of wallpaper removed from the dining room sported soldiers clad in war garb aiming muskets with attached bayonets, rifles, and pistols. It was a totally bizarre ambience for dining, but it may have been a tribute or memorial to the men who fought in the Revolutionary War or the War of 1812.

Removing the carpet and pad in the thirty-by-fifteen-square foot living room exposed the most beautiful one-and-one-half inch tongue-and-groove oak hardwood floors. I wonder if most people are as ignorant as I was of the physical toll men and women undergo when they choose one of the remodeling professions. I doubt I have ever been so physically exhausted. Muscles roared all over my body, especially while I was removing the carpet, pad, and staples from the floors of the 3,100 square foot house.

The workers and I cut carpet and pads into manageable pieces with a utility knife and rolled, carried, and tossed years of nasty grime into the big dumpster outside by the barn. My arm strength probably came from hoeing, cheerleading, and mowing. I was able to sit and kneel on the floor and pull hundreds of staples in preparation for the floor man. Once that job was done, I had no desire to ever hold a pair of pliers for an extended length of time. The blisters on my hands did eventually heal.

Removal of the chair lift to the upstairs rooms posed a massive challenge. Five layers of carpet covered the oak staircase. Pulling out the long

spikes from the back of each step took amazing strength and persever-
ance. It was a job I had to pass along to the men.

Removing the wallpaper and old lights from the upstairs ceiling not
only uncovered cracked plaster, but also revealed a leaky roof. Yellow
water sloshed about when we removed one of the round ceiling light
fixtures in the master bedroom. Again, it was a layering scenario. This old
house had a total of seven roofs. Welcome roofers to our party!

My life routine grew old, and I started to covet Mac's life. He could
dress up, go to work, come by the farm to inspect projects, then go home.
He got to play with William, read a bedtime story, watch the news, drink
a highball, and go to bed early. Weariness got me.

The den had been covered with dark wood paneling that hid built-in
cabinets, bookshelves, and a fireplace. Mac always loved treasure hunting. He rummaged through the barn in search of the missing fireplace
mantel. Excited with a find, he pulled me away from cleaning the kitchen
one Saturday to show me the original screen doors, complete with their
wooden Victorian gingerbread. Looking through the screens propped up
against the barn wall, I spied his treasure.

"Bill, those doors are great," I remarked, "but I love the oak wood
fireplace mantel even more." We called in a brick mason who helped
restore the castaway mantel to its intended place and purpose. The reborn
mantel transformed the den from bleak and dim to brilliant and inviting.

The day our wrought-iron security doors were installed, I received a
quick lesson on the importance of pushing in the button to keep from
locking yourself out of the house. Later the same day, a plumber rang
the doorbell and I rushed from the kitchen to greet him. William was
napping in the upstairs bedroom and I didn't want the doorbell to wake
him. The door closed and locked behind me. My heart skipped a beat. I
looked at the plumber eyes wide, mouth gaping.

I confessed my predicament to the seven-foot-tall plumber. Staring up at him in earnest, I pleaded. "If I get a ladder from the garage,

would you mind getting on the roof? See that window without a screen? If you break the pane with a hammer, you could climb in the house and open my door."

The plumber shook his head, eyes darting everywhere but my way. "Sorry," he said, "but I'm afraid of heights."

"Really?" I wondered how on earth the man got out of bed in the morning. All I could think about was William. If he woke up and no one came when he called out, he'd feel like his mom left him.

"If I get a ladder, would you mind holding it while I climb the roof?"

"That, I can do," he said, plainly relieved.

Rushing to the barn, I stuck a hammer in my sweatshirt pocket, grabbed a pair of garden gloves, and clumsily carried the ladder to the porch by the kitchen. Like a professional roofer, I marched up each rung and successfully got on the flat porch roof and carefully made my way to the portion with the steepest pitch. I only focused on the window, not the ground. Hammer in hand, I carefully smashed the middle pane by the window lock and removed the glass. Fortunately, the lock flipped, and the window opened with a few jerks as I broke into my own house while William slept on.

I called Mac to confess. "Mac, the security doors are installed, and the wrought iron is beautiful. They even come with screens. There is one tiny problem. We've had a break in."

"What?" Mac said. "What happened?"

"Well," I said slowly to milk anticipation. "We'll need to replace a window in the upstairs bedroom."

"You mean to tell me someone broke in an upstairs bedroom window? Did they use a ladder?"

"A ladder and a hammer. Yep, that's exactly what I used."

"You?"

"Mac, I guess I proved security doors really work."

Mac laughed.

Taking risks is unnatural for me. My memory bank overflows with the faces of patients and families living with the results of a bad fall. One man I encountered had dated a girl a few times and was helping put a new roof on a barn for her family when he fell and broke his neck. It left him a quadriplegic with little use of his arms; we nurses were heart-broken for all involved. A bad fall has the capacity to slam life into the dirt, and even when help arrives and moves you to the emergency room, some degree of personal independence remains diminished. Maybe the plumber knew stories like this too, for his sister was a nurse. Truth be known, I was just as afraid of falling as he was afraid of heights.

After several months, the house became a beautiful showplace inside and out as I found peace in my home, my glory land, my blooms, birds, and gardens. Everything I learned from Gram and Grandpa, I applied to my life with gusto. I bought a little tiller and made gardens. I grew columbine, pink and purple cups and saucers from seed. I planted lark-spur, delphinium, and every dahlia bulb Burpee sold. I grew foxglove and taught little William how to plant and water the gardens. I used the push mower around the house and trimmed, just like I did when I lived with Grandpa.

One Saturday, Mac came out into the side yard while I was mowing and said, "Let me push mow a row." He did one strip. He had no love for outdoor work. As far as gardening, Mac's dad had a man to manage his vegetable garden, so I always attributed his apathy to a lack of experience. Me, on the other hand, I loved to can green beans and tomatoes, freeze corn, cook, and bake, remembering all Gram had taught me.

We bought the farm in October of 1987, the same month the stock market fell flat. Bill stressed, but we got over it. His dad helped us a lot in those days, but I never knew. By 1988 we were happy and loving the country life, until I got a call from Gram.

Chapter 23:

If You Come Home and Take Care of Me, I Know I'll Get Well

A bout two years had passed since Grandpa died, and Gram developed difficulty breathing and was diagnosed with heart failure. That meant another trip to Pennsylvania, only this time little William stayed behind with his dad and the McCutchans. It was hard to leave the sweetest boy in the world even for a couple days, let alone a week.

The night before I left for Pennsylvania, an old friend from Khaletown church called me. "Donna, this is Blanche Horneman. Today the doctors transferred your grandmother from Brookville to a University Hospital in Pittsburgh. By chance, does your plane stop in Pittsburgh?"

"Yes, it does."

"Well just get off and Jerry will pick you up and we will meet you at the hospital. Then the two of you can stay with Augie and me, we don't live far."

Blanche and Augie, church friends from my high school days, lightened up any potluck with jokes and stories. What a blessing to know I would be surrounded with friends, as my adventure included forced time with Gram's new husband, Jerry.

Gram had met this Jerry guy at church and married him secretly about a year after Grandpa died. I couldn't have picked him out of a lineup. I had never had a one-on-one conversation with him. When I arrived at the Pittsburgh airport, the saying "first impressions are irretrievable" came true.

As I sat alone in the dimly-lit lower level of the Landside Terminal my adrenalin sharpened all of my senses. The steady "clunk, clunk, clunk, clunk" of the empty ever-rolling luggage carousel belt was the only sound. It was moving aimlessly, serving no purpose; all of the recent passengers had snatched up their luggage hours ago, including me. I watched two figures approaching, a security guard and a slow-walking man. I soon found slow to be his consistent attribute. Everyone has at least one. We walked—slowly—out to his car.

"Thanks, Jerry, for picking me up," I said. "How's Gram doing?"

Tossing my luggage into his trunk, he fumbled to find the keys in his pocket. "I hope okay," he replied. The major feat before us was finding our way to the cardiac specialty hospital from the airport parking lot. I had prepared a detailed route plan with marked exits, approximate mileage, and maps of the city in my purse. He took the driver's seat, and trouble took the wheel.

"Jerry, you need to get in the right lane."

"No, I can't do that."

"Jerry, turn your turn signal on and give it some gas, there is no one behind you, you have room, quick get in the right lane."

"No. I can't go over 30 miles an hour. This is a strange town. I don't want to get a ticket."

I found it impossible to camouflage my frustration, I yelled at Gram's newlywed husband, "Jerry, you're taking us in the opposite direction!" And then I shut up. I watched in amazement as he bumbled to himself, turning this way and that with no plan, no map, and no idea how dangerous it was to crawl through strange neighborhoods. After forty-five minutes, I spied a gas station and blurted, "Pull over at that gas station or I will get out and walk."

He pulled over.

Luckily a customer at the gas station gave me specific directions to the hospital from our location and added, "This is not a good part of town for a woman to be driving about lost!" I had figured as much as I saw people gathered in groups near chain link fences, smoking, drinking, and heaven only knows what else.

I filled the car with gas and encouraged Jerry to use the facilities. I sat like a concrete statue in the driver's seat. Knocking on my window, he said, "I'm driving, move. This is my car."

"I am driving. Keys please." Eyes wide, mouth gaping, he surrendered, but his tongue never did. The car ran well over thirty. Driving in cities has never bothered me. I had driven from North Carolina to Pennsylvania multiple times. I followed my directions carefully right to the hospital.

Blanche and Augie smiled when we walked into Gram's room, and there were hugs all around. "Where have you been?" asked Blanche.

Smirking, I said, "taking a tour of the town. Just glad to be here, Gram." I brushed off the Jerry incident as I brushed Gram's hair and heard about the ambulance ride and the multitude of future tests scheduled over the next few days. We left that evening, and I suggested Jerry ride with Augie, so Blanche and I could chatter. Anytime we needed to get to and from the hospital, I drove. Jerry hated every moment, but he didn't have a choice.

Gram suffered from a heart valve problem. Valve disease is like a door that doesn't open or close properly. When heart chambers fill and squeeze blood volume some valves close tight while others open, ensuring the forward flow of blood. Calcium deposits had made her valves inefficient, creating high pressure in her lungs. Her ineffective heart pump was unable to handle the backflow. She had been in and out of the hospital multiple times, unable to breathe.

Gram had never learned to drive a car, but when it came time to making personal health decisions, she never lost her way. Her compass stayed spot on. Once test results came in, persuasion pressure began. The reason for Gram's transfer from a small community hospital to a university setting was simple—she met the criteria for a research study. The intervention being studied involved inserting a catheter into the patient's groin, threading it through vessels into her heart, and inflating a balloon to bust apart the calcium deposits on her tight valves. Dottie was the perfect research rat. Or so they thought.

"Dottie, I'm Mark, a resident here at the university hospital," the good-looking fellow with a crisp virgin lab coat announced as he scooted his chair close to her bed. "Have you signed your consent yet?" Every few hours a med student, resident, or department chief wooed, joked, bargained with, and charmed the uneducated, white-haired 78-year-old. One resident placed his stethoscope in Dottie's ears to listen to her loud heart murmur. Gram couldn't have known normal heart sounds, let alone a murmur. Identify the bird songs of an orange tanager or rose-breasted grosbeak, you betcha. Heart murmurs? Never.

Looking like a country bumpkin full of ignorance and total disinterest, my grandmother basked in their attention. She smiled like a flirting teenager, shook her head "no," and threw back her shoulders to sit up as tall as a four-foot-eleven-inch frame could in order to accentuate her best attribute—that 44-inch bust. Gram always said what she meant and meant what she said. The university research team soon discovered one tough bird hidden under the guise of a little old woman.

Exasperated by the inability of his team to enlist Dottie as a participant in the study, the head researcher stormed into her room, his lab coat whipping about with every stride. Loaded with logic, facts, and threats, he stood over her with arms crossed and a stern face, peering over glasses about to fall off his nose. This doctor delivered a heartless persuasion speech.

"Dottie, you are going to die in a very short amount of time. This procedure is risky, but it may give you a better quality of life. You may live longer and have more endurance. If you don't survive the procedure, so what? You're going to die very soon anyway."

I sat on the bed beside Gram and slipped my hand into hers. I gave it a gentle squeeze. That simple action belonged to Gram, her nonverbal "I love you so much" whenever she held your hand. In this uncomfortable moment, it was my turn to squeeze love.

The physician rambled on. "What better legacy to leave your loved ones than helping others through research? You can be responsible for saving God knows how many through your sacrifice. How about signing your consent and we can do this procedure this afternoon?"

Gram smiled. She absorbed every spoken word, totally unbothered to know that death was sure to pounce any minute. Pulling the shawl collar of her robe high around her neck, Gram's glare surfaced. "I'm not signing that consent."

The researcher threw his arms high in the air, shaking empty hands as if he were crying to God for heavenly revelation manna "Why not?"

Tapping on the three-inch-high investigational research consent on her bedside table she said, "I read it."

"You read what?"

"I read the consent."

"The whole thing?"

"Yes, and it says in there if I have this procedure, I could have a stroke, so I'm not signing."

"Oh, Dottie, a stroke isn't so bad. People live with strokes all the time. That should not stop you, for this is a once in a lifetime hope for you."

"I'm not signing. My sister, Mary, is in a nursing home in a catatonic condition and has suffered many strokes."

"Dottie, just think of what a burden you are to your family. You go back and forth to the hospital all the time."

"Well, if you think I'm a burden now, just how much of a burden do you think I'll be when I have a stroke?"

"Okay, okay, Dottie, then there is nothing more we can do for you. I'll write discharge orders and you can go home within the hour."

Uncomfortable and disappointing as it must have been, the researchers surrendered the health care keys, and Gram drove herself in the exact direction she wanted to go. These professionals knew much about Dottie's physical malady, but they did not know Gram.

She loved to read. She read the *Grit* newspaper, poetry, and her Bible every night aloud—very loud, because Grandpa was hard of hearing and refused to wear his hearing aids. Her voice vibrated through the walls of the tiny house. I know this to be true. When Gram read to Grandpa, she read to me. I am certain she read every word of the consent.

I drove Gram home, turning on the radio to deafen my response button to Jerry, who perched in the front seat. "How fast are you going?" he asked anxiously. Leaning over to read the speedometer, he said "It looks like you're speeding. You're going to get a ticket."

"If I get a ticket, it is my responsibility."

"No ma'am, you are in my car."

Potential smart phrases flooded my mind, but I kept my mouth shut tight. You can't fix stupid, there is no vaccine. You can't change anyone but yourself. Some suffer from constipation of the mind and diarrhea of the mouth. But this man was Gram's new husband, and he was sweet to her. She wasn't alone. He wasn't Grandpa and never could be. She must have seen something good in him.

As soon as we got home Gram begged me, "Would you please help me take a bath and scrub my head, I need to wash the hospital off me.

They didn't have a bathtub." I've probably bathed hundreds or thousands of strangers over the years, but the humility meter busts when you're bathing your own frail, wrinkled, proud Grandma who loved to stay "fersh" and clean.

Carefully helping her to step out of the tub, I helped her dry, dress, and stay warm. We made our way to the living room couch, and I dried her hair. I propped up pillows, elevating her legs and feet on the rose-embroidered footstool.

I then hustled about the kitchen to make a saltless, tasteless supper. A heart failure diet restricts salt because it causes water retention. Gram watched me from the couch, and she couldn't stand it. We had always cooked together in the cramped little kitchen. She must have felt like a prisoner in a body that had stalled. Any exertion took her breath away.

"Donna, come here. Is this going to be my life? Sitting watching others do for me? I should be in the kitchen fixing your favorite meal of ham loaf, scalloped potatoes, and coleslaw. What is really wrong with me?"

"Gram, you have a heart valve that doesn't open or close well because of calcium. So, fluid backs up in your lungs and pressure builds up. It's called heart failure; the pump is tired. For seventy-eight years your heart faithfully beat 60-100 times per minute."

"Well, if my heart worked well all these years, why is it stopping now?"

Sometimes, no amount of explanation or education can serve up understanding to a person suffering loss of quality of life. Gram ate little of her supper. Graciously, she pushed bland meatloaf, mashed taters, and lima beans round and round. She decided to head to bed and called it a day. She and Jerry slept in my old bedroom because it was closest to the bathroom.

I quickly cleaned the kitchen and got ready for bed. Sleeping in Grandpa and Grandma's old bedroom was the oddest feeling in the whole world. The last time I had slept in this bed was with Patti Marie during Grandpa's funeral two years earlier.

As I pulled down the covers, I was stopped by an ominous feeling. The rattle of heart failure resonated through the walls, drawing me to Gram's door.

I knocked, "Gram?"

Jerry said, "Come in."

Cradled in Jerry's short chubby arms, Gram struggled with every breath despite four pillows elevating her shoulders and head.

"Gram, I think we need to go to the hospital."

Reaching for me, she cupped my face with her hands and studied my weariness, saying "No, not yet. Honey, you look so tired. Please get some sleep."

We exchanged cheek kisses and "I love yous" and I scurried to the other side of the house, practically dove into bed and sent God the most intense emergent prayer of my life. "Father, I am exhausted. I know a trip to the hospital is coming. I need to sleep hard and fast. Please, please, please make it happen for me. Please."

My head hit the pillow and I slept until Jerry pounded on the door, snapped on the blazing overhead light, and screamed "Donna, get up. The ambulance is on its way. I'll ride with Dottie." He threw his car keys on the dresser. "You take my car. Hurry up."

Two hours of sleep felt like twelve. "Thank you, Lord."

The emergency room physician examined Gram and looked at us. "She won't make it through the night. She is almost nonresponsive." Jerry and I walked alongside the gurney as they wheeled her to a semi-private room. I met her nurse. She remembered me from high school.

"Your grandmother has an infection, and we won't be putting anyone in this room. Feel free to sleep in this other bed tonight."

I had notified Mom and her brother, my uncle Rodger, who came later that night. Jerry went back home, and I took the night shift. Sleeping in a hospital bed is hard to do as a patient. It's harder with a loved one rattling with each breath in the next bed. I jumped up to respond to the shrill of a code blue call over the PA system around 4:30 a.m. then realized this was not my hospital.

Around 6:00 a.m. I washed my face and brushed my hair in the bathroom. Gram turned her head and opened her eyes, "Donna, what are you doing?"

"Washing up a bit and pulling my hair up in a ponytail."

Totally awake from her coma, she asked "Do you think you could do something with my hair?"

And Gram was back. The ER doctor was wrong. Over the next few months visits to the hospital increased, just like the research doctor predicted.

For Gram's final hospitalization Mom called Patti Marie to go with her. Patti declined and Mom got snarly. Thank God that Mom decided to go anyway. Mom and Gram spent the day looking at magazines and talking, and even ate lunch together. A great mother-daughter day ended with a late-night call from Gram's nurse.

"Your mother has gone to sleep, and she won't be waking up again.

Chapter 24:

Divorce: My Shameful Mark of Failure

G randma's death meant another trip to Pennsylvania alone with William—and without my husband.

It was odd to be in the town I called home during high school with no home to go to. We all thought Gram's little white house belonged to Jerry. The out-of-towners, Mom, Uncle Rodger, Patti Marie, and I got a block of rooms at the little old inn.

Just one day into this mess, William got very sick with a high fever, and I never felt so helpless. He slept most of the day. I didn't have a car. My pediatrician might as well have been in another country. I didn't have a phone or medicine. Any mother gets hit with waves of terror, but a nurse thinks the worst. Years ago, I saved a baby's life. I diagnosed a little one with bacterial meningitis. William reminded me of him, a limp and lifeless rag doll.

When Mom got to the inn that night, she helped me take William to the ER. I probably looked like a lowlife—no makeup, no sleep, old shirt and jeans. The physician didn't want to treat him. We were out-of-towners with Indiana insurance. Fear of non-payment trumped any professional courtesy. He nearly walked out of the room dismissing the illness as minor when William threw up all over the gurney and caught his attention.

Finally, the ER physician caved and examined my son. I helped to hold William still while the doctor peered into his ears with the otoscope. "Wow, nasty ear infections, both ears." He ordered antibiotics and told us there would be no flying anytime soon. I thanked God one nightmare could be put to bed. What an ending that was to an exhausting day, not just for me, but for Mom.

After the funeral, Mom and Uncle Rodger dealt with poor Jerry. He kept reciting all the important things he and Gram had put in their will. He scurried around Gram's desk, shuffling through documents and sifting through check registers, until Mom and Uncle Rodger discovered the thrilling truth. The will Jerry and Gram had composed was written with the invisible ink of good intentions. They had never made one. I thanked God that Grandpa's attorney had secured the only will—my grandparents' original.

Everything belonged to Mom and Uncle Rodger, and yet they stood by and allowed Jerry to take things that did not belong to him. Why that old man wrapped and packed piece after piece of Gram's green and ruby colored depression glassware from the corner shelves in the living room, I will never know. Now and then Mom or Rodger cautiously said, "Now Jerry, I think that's enough." The man kept on packing glass until Rodger stepped between him and the shelving.

This situation changed my philosophy concerning after-death distribution of personal stuff. I believe it is best to give things to those you love while you are still alive. Jerry opened Gram's cedar chest and gave nearly all of her handmade quilts to his own granddaughter. I wanted to scream "Leave some for me!" But Mom and Uncle Rodger stood by quietly and so did I. They let him give not one, not two, but all of Gram's quilts to someone who never even held her hand. I went out to the flower garden and cried.

Gram's funeral was such a contrast to Grandpa's. His funeral was packed, while hers was slim in numbers. She had outlived many of family members and friends. At the grave site, reality sank in. Often in our lives we say or think these words: "I can never come home again." My grandparents were gone, and the homestead and garage sold quickly. I knew I needed to make the McCutchanville farm my home.

I tried to do just that, and I failed miserably. I remember that when I lived in North Carolina, a friend's marriage had fallen to pieces. Her advice to me was, "Donna, you're single. I know loneliness is hard, but married and lonely is horrible."

I doubt I understood it at the time, but when I stood in her shoes, I knew she was right. Loneliness is never more alive than when three loved ones die, and your husband never shows. I am sure my Pennsylvania family and friends probably wondered if I really had a husband. At least he did drive to Pennsylvania to take us back to Indiana, if only because of William's ear infections.

Months later, one of Mac's relatives died, a nurse who none of the family ever talked about and whom I had never met. Mac took off several vacation days to drive his parents to her funeral. My husband was always on call for his mother and father and son, but never for me. I told Mac how hurtful this was to me, but he didn't get it. Mac bragged about being in Mensa, which confused me. How can a man with a high IQ be so obtuse?

Perhaps we both were basket cases. We lived in people-pleasing silos. Mac tried to please his parents and his boss while I tried to please him. On an innocent fall day in 1988, reality ran over me when Mac and I walked down the paved drive to get the mail.

I asked him "What do you want with my life?" Mac glanced my way. "Huh?" He picked up a stick from the driveway, walked across the front yard and tossed it into the woods.

A still small voice deep inside me answered, "It's your life, your life, your life."

Walking back to the house alone I watched the oak leaves drop from the faithful old trees that lined the drive. Leaves know when it's time to go. So did I.

My life was mine.

Chapter 25:

Over and Done

About a week later, I visited Freddie while Mac worked. A friend babysat William. After greeting me with a smile, Freddie ushered me to my familiar chair and handed me a bottle of water. "I'm glad you called," he said. "I'm anxious to hear how things are going for you and Bill and William."

"Bill and William are healthy and happy," I said, fiddling with my wedding band. "My marriage isn't either of those. I am so tired of the way Mrs. McCutchan treats me. She puts me down every chance she gets. I can't take it anymore. Mac will never support me. I refused to go to their Easter dinner, and you would think World War III began."

Freddie stopped me. "Donna, why not attend a family Easter celebration?"

"I love Jesus, they don't. I refused to be the target of hateful atheistic jeers, especially on resurrection Sunday." I reached for my water, took a drink, then spilled a hidden truth. "I never told anyone but, when I was a kid, Rip used to do the same thing—make fun of my faith."

Leaning forward, eyebrows raised, Freddie asked, "What does Bill do? He's a Christian."

"Is he? I wonder about that sometimes."

Freddie said, "Donna, what makes you wonder?"

Shrugging, I said, "One night during a spat, he sat up in bed and with a desperate tone he growled at me. 'Don't you think for one minute I don't want what you have?' Freddie, to this day, I have no idea what he was talking about. The fact he never crossed his family or stood up for his faith makes me wonder. I really love Mac's cousin Ken, but he gets on a rampage when it comes to Jesus. Last year he ranted, 'Jesus isn't really God. He never died, never rose from the dead, the disciples rolled away the stone, stole his body and fashioned the greatest mockery in history.' Then he added, 'Only spineless people believe this fairytale.'"

Freddie shook his head.

"Of course," I continued, "Aunt Bettye's head bobbed in agreement, elbows on the table, leaning forward, sucking on a cigarette and intentionally spewing smoke at the Christian, me."

Searching for an answer, I looked intently at Freddie. "Do you think these rich people hate my guts? Is it a game to them to ridicule me? They don't believe in Christ crucified, but they sure don't hold back crucifying me."

Before he had a chance to get a word in, I rattled on. "After last year's experience, I put my foot down. My family went to church, had a nice meal, and then gardened. Bill and I planted yellow marigolds while William played in the backyard. Bill stayed home with me, but it totally unnerved him to cross the McCutchans."

Freddie took off his glasses and leaned deep into his overstuffed chair. "Donna you're a McCutchan."

"No. Never have been. Never will be. And truthfully, I never want to be anything like those people. Freddie, I am so sorry. I tried. I failed."

I was relieved to finally take a deep breath after unlatching the prison door that kept my true feelings in solitary confinement, and I waited pensively for Freddie to respond. With a cross between a smile, a smirk, and a frown, Freddy leaned back into his overstuffed chair, patted the armrests twice, clapped his hands, and announced, "Donna Dee you are mad. I have never seen you so mad. Donna, it's over. Get out. Don't bother with separation. Go straight to divorce."

Divorce! The dreaded shameful mark of failure I had never wanted embroidered on my life. A wave of relief came gently over me as Freddie's word pictures taught me well.

"People understand physical abuse, black eyes, bruises, broken bones," he said. "Emotional abuse is just as painful, maybe more so, for it leads to deep internal wounds and soul scars requiring extra time for healing."

I imagined a trauma victim with purple swollen eyes, cast-covered arms, a leg in traction, and black and blue bruises on the back from being kicked repeatedly.

"Outsiders cannot see evidence of the beating and will be baffled trying to understand your choice to leave a prominent rich man's son. You are amiable, and young enough to have a happy life. I counsel a woman who stayed in an emotionally abusive situation sacrificing any chance for a fulfilling life for the sake of the children. Now misery and bitterness hold her day and night— nasty partners for the last chapter of life. Get out. Do it for yourself and for your son. Your purpose, according to the McCutchans, was to elevate Mac."

The family's animosity toward me escalated when the McCutchans found out I wanted to leave. Anger and social embarrassment blinded them. They continued to punch and pound with fists of hateful words and slap me with sick solutions that only succeeded in validating my difficult decision. The efforts Mac's parents used to change my mind more than surprised me—they offended me terribly. The persuasion stick replaced the carrot with money. Mac's dad asked him to relay this solution: "Tell Donna, I'll gladly provide a monthly stipend of $1,000 if she forgets the divorce and stays."

Mrs. McCutchan included a $1000 check with the ugliest letter on her lovely cream monogrammed stationery. "You should have been an actress..." It was the only letter and check I ever destroyed after reading it. I called her. "Mrs. McCutchan, thanks but you need to know I ripped up your check. I wanted you to know so you can keep your bank register straight."

During this stressful time, their housekeeper confided in me. Mrs. McCutchan signed out a pile of library books about divorce in search of answers. Divorce, to her, seemed like a dreaded disease I carried, and now the McCutchan family was infected too. She told the housekeeper, "Well, Donna is the product of a divorced family. That has to be the reason for all of this."

The housekeeper shared her thoughts with me. "Donna, I so wanted to remind her that when she married Harold, she married a divorced man.

Another suggestion from Mac's dad involved infidelity: "Tell her to have an affair and get it out of her system." I knew better than to dive under a blanket of infidelity. Little did they know, Mac was the only man enticing me to leave. He placed a ring on my finger, whispered vows in my ears, and ignited hope in my heart.

But hope left. Vows vanished. Emotional abuse remained.

Chapter 26:

No Value

Divorce. A friend once told me no person walks down the aisle and makes forever promises in a church before family, friends, and God with thoughts of divorce dancing in the ballroom of their mind. I believe that to be true. As one who came from a divorced family, I held a deep aversion to the D-word and the despicable process it represented, but I filed anyway. It was probably the hardest decision I have ever made.

Yet, ugly attitudes and unkind words chased away my doubts. The day of our hearing in divorce court, I entered the assigned conference room to meet with my attorney. Three men in suits stood talking in the corner by the window, discussing the case. Mac's attorney shared his concerns with Mac and Larry, my attorney. "Essentially," he said, "Donna brought absolutely nothing into this marriage."

I bit my lip. If only I were a sassy brat, I'd have finished his sentence for him. "…and you will be sure, I will carry nothing out." Mac nodded, acknowledging my presence while his attorney continued to devalue my existence. The attorneys turned, saw me, and as if I were deaf, rambled on. My one previous request provided fodder for their discussion of financial investments (or the lack thereof).

About a month before, I had laid out one demand. I needed a complete compilation of all of Mac's financial holdings for the five years we were married. He had never shared any of this with me. I thought that if in the future my son ever wondered why I left his father, he could read this document.

Mac provided it for me, in the form of multiple pages on legal sheets that read like a tot fighting over toys in kindergarten. "This pharmaceutical stock is mine. My father started this fund when I was born. My coin collection belongs to me. My mutual funds, my retirement account, my insurance, my Toyota Supra, my furniture, my farm, and my property. All of it is mine."

Mac and I crafted much of the property settlement together in the living room of the farm in order to save attorney fees. Mac pleaded with me every time he saw me. "Please keep your hands off my profit sharing, it's my best investment. Please don't touch my retirement." My goal in life never included busting him financially. I did as he wished and never touched the precious investment he loved so.

During the hearing, I sat in that courtroom and thought of all I brought into the marriage. One night in anger, Mac let it slip. "Don't you think for a minute I knew when I married you how much nurses make?" Count one. Mark my education and earning power valuable. Count two. William. No need to count further. He, or maybe his dad, gave me $50,000, and William and I lived at the farm for free. He agreed to give me a monthly stipend of $500.

Mac and I walked out together, and I asked, "Why couldn't you love me?" Sheepishly, he looked down at his glossy black shoes. "I did." Then he winked and added, "I'm going to be the best ex-husband in Vanderburgh County."

"Oh Mac, you got that totally backwards. Your resolve to be the best never showed up during our marriage. Now with divorce, it magically appears? I won't hold my breath."

And we went our separate ways.

Chapter 27:

Loving the Little People

D ivorce is like stepping on a bee in bare feet. The fuzzy little critter stops you in your tracks, creates unforgettable pain, and you've got a temporary limp, at least until the stinger is removed. When my divorce was finalized, I stepped up my game. I enrolled in school, worked every weekend, and enjoyed the freedom to be myself.

Friends introduced me to John Bradshaw's tape series on the family system theory. Dr. Bradshaw described children as little people with video cameras recording their parents' actions, behaviors, and words for future play, when they become parents themselves. One alarming truth I discovered is that some tapes are blank. Mac's were. Mine featured dysfunction.

After absorbing Dr. Bradshaw's videos and books for months in 1989 and 1990, I changed. The knowledge I gained from this examination of family systems replaced blame, shame, and despair with a resolve to give William recordings worth watching. I deliberately took every opportunity to make memories, good ones.

One May morning, when William and I walked to the car to go to preschool, he stopped. Eyes shiny, voice trembling, "Oh Mommy, I'm all wet."

"William, no problem," I said. I quickly unlocked the side porch door. "I'll draw bath water and you can wash off quick. I'll get you clean clothes and we will still get to school on time." It was the quickest bath that boy ever took. On the way to school I calmly said, "William, you know accidents happen. You did nothing wrong."

Later that week while doing dishes, I dropped my favorite pottery milk pitcher, a gift from my friend Paula from North Carolina. I busted it to pieces on the old porcelain sink. Then I gave myself a loud verbal beating unaware my little person heard every word. "Dang, Donna. Stupid, stupid, stupid. You should have been more careful." Fighting back tears, I cried "I'll never have another."

A little hand patted my arm. "Mommy, it's okay. Don't cry. Accidents happen." Little people learn a lesson and teach the teacher. He taught me often.

One evening during Halloween I sat on the living room floor cutting out a Raggedy Andy costume. I tossed balls of wadded up brown tissue paper from cutting out the pattern pieces all over the floor. Piles of red, white, and blue fabric scraps, my pin cushions, scissors, and weights were spread out all around me. On the other side of the living room, William watched TV surrounded by his Brio train, Legos, books, art pads, and markers.

Glancing up from my project, I said, "William, please pick up your mess. You don't need all those toys out on the floor."

Obedient and quiet, he gathered armloads of toys and deposited them adjacent to my scraps and pattern pieces. "William, what are you doing?" I asked.

"Mommy, I'm putting my mess with yours."

My little person taught me the definition of mess differs from mess maker to mess maker. Together we picked up the living room. We did a lot together in the preschool and elementary years.

William helped me in the kitchen a lot. He made homemade biscuits with me and cheered me on when I baked entrees for the county fair. One July, after working late the night before, I furiously made ginger snaps, pies, rolls, and cornbread. A moment of panic arose. The cornbread held onto the pan and refused to let go. William studied my every move as I tried to persuade the spatula to free the bread. No give. I looked at William and said, "I think I'll just throw it against the wall." "Not a good idea, Mommy." Finally, it gave, but it broke into pieces on the paper plate.

"Well, I guess I'm not entering those crumbs." William grabbed up the plate, carefully put it in a plastic bag, sealed it and said, "We're taking this anyway. It's not about looks. It's about taste." How can a kid be so spot on? Our cornbread won a Grand Champion purple ribbon. It was totally his win.

I decided to go back to school and work on my professional career. Juggling the roles of mother, student, nurse, and Sunday school teacher opened up a greater world for me and William. Our group of friends expanded, and William flourished. Every few months from 1990 through 1995, the farm became a great place for pitch-in dinners and outdoor parties that always included entire families. I worked hard on food prep, but when the gang showed up, I always played with the kids.

One of my friends told me I had missed my calling. "Donna," she said, "you should be a children's activity director for a cruise line." Creating fun out of the simplest things came easy for me. I bought large stiff sheets of white paper and a bucket of markers, crayons, and colored pencils.

I gathered the kids on the front porch and handed them paper and told them, "Each of you own an airplane. I'll help you make it, but you need to design it and learn how to fly." And all the kids, ages five through twelve, chattered, giggled, and made amazing colorful planes. Then we had contests to see how far their planes flew, marking the landings with sticks from the woods.

Fall parties included distributing rakes to excited kids so they could transform thick piles of leaves into intricate mazes and play a crazy version of freezer tag called "witch in the well". The witch captured little children and put them in the big leaf pile designated the "well." Leaving the prisoners unattended, the "witch" ran down the maze to catch more innocent children. Meanwhile kids ran from the witch while others freed the prisoners.

Running wildly through a leaf maze on a crisp fall day is a great memory maker. For a parent that's important, but memory-making is a two-way street.

William's friend John came to play one sunny day. I gave them sheets and clothespins to make tents on the clothesline. I knew these two indus-trious seven-year-old boys could safely be trusted to make their own fun. I spent the morning cleaning the upstairs and decided I might capture a video moment of the boys. I walked out on the back porch and said, "Hey John, what have you been doing this morning?"

John smiled and danced excitedly about. "We are makin' a cwistal pawlace. Let me show you." Pointing to every clothespin (he had about twenty holding the sheets together), he proudly said, "Here's a cwistal, here's a cwistal…" I kept taping and asked, "John, what's in the pawlace?"

"Oh, we are playin' wobbers. Here, I'll show you." Taking off some clothespins to get into the tent, he quickly closed the sheet door behind him. He displayed the stolen items one at a time by sticking his arm out of the tent.

"We wobbed this"—my blue and white vase from the sitting room. "We wobbed this"—my blue speckled roaster pan from the kitchen cab-inet. "John, do you mind if I look inside the cwistal pawlace?" I asked.

Shrugging, John looked across the driveway at William for advice. What a sight that was! Running like the Tasmanian devil across the drive-way, William pushed a plastic orange and yellow grocery cart filled with "wobbery" items into a huge pile of leaves and crashed and burned. He looked like a cross between Superman and a gnome. On his head was his thick, monogrammed terrycloth baby towel. Once he rose out of the leaf pile, he took the edges of his towel cape and wildly tried to whip the leaves off like a bird flapping his wings. Then he did another run.

John and I looked at him, then at each other. John smiled. "I guess that's okay."

Clumsily balancing the huge video recorder on my right shoulder, I continued recording the loot collected by my little wobbers. Inside the tent were my couch cushions from the living room, two lamps, a plant from the side porch, and more kitchen utensils. I got it all on tape.

Working weekends enabled me to be off and help with school parties or be a chaperone for outings. On Valentine's Day when William was in elementary school, I volunteered to help with the sweetheart party. I joined a happy, chatty group of mothers, but when I introduced myself, their attitude changed. "Oh, so you're William's mother?"

Nodding my head with motherly pride and great expectations of positive comments, acknowledged, "Yes, I am."

A dark-headed mother glanced at her friends as if to gather moral courage and started the conversation. "We really need to talk to you."

Sensing a serious issue, I said, "Okay."

The blonde blurted. "William has all the girls."

"What?" I didn't dare laugh, for these five women stood tall, arms crossed, jaws fixed with determination.

The redhead nodded. "She's right, you know. I came to have lunch with my son in the cafeteria and there was a whole table full of boys. The other table by the windows, had all of the girls and William."

Like a visitor attending a meeting of match-making mothers' misery I listened intently, nodded, and said little. Near tears, one mother said, "My son has a crush on Mallory, and she won't have anything to do with him. But she talks to William all the time."

Once the unloading of motherly frustration was complete, I felt sorry for these broken-hearted boys and their mothers. I tried to imagine how competing with that good-looking blue-eyed Casanova named

William McCutchan day after day made these little boys feel. It had to be depressing. Then revelation smacked me.

"First," I told them, "You do realize this is elementary school. I doubt your sons will suffer any permanent emotional damage. What you don't know is many of the girls in this class have known William for years. Several attended the same preschool, and many go to our church, where I teach Sunday school. In a way they grew up together." I could easily have added, "But of course, his smashing personality, his sense of humor, his kind heart, and the fact that his grandad is a millionaire may give him an advantage." But I kept those words behind locked lips.

A look of relief fell over the other mothers. It seemed the thought of William and the girls engaging in a brotherly and sisterly relationship settled concerns.

During these single-parenting years William went to the McCutchans every weekend while I worked. Bill lived with his parents, five minutes from the farm. Children from divorce often end up moved about from house to house. One divorced friend asked her son, "Where is home?" Sitting cross legged on his bed, the little boy stopped coloring, cocked his head, and smiled. "That's easy, Momma. Home is where your toys are." I think William felt the same.

I like to think home is where love lives. And for William love was in both places.

Chapter 28:

Stick and Stitches

Mrs. McCutchan enjoyed entertaining William and his friends, especially after the death of her husband on New Year's Day in 1995. She had cared for him at home with home health care and the help of her sister. During this same time, she was diagnosed with early-stage dementia. I felt sorry for her losses, and I knew William gave her joy.

Later in January of that year, during William's birthday week, a snowstorm blanketed the paths in the woods behind her house and created perfect sledding conditions. She called and persuaded me to let William stay over one more day to sled with his friend Robert. I agreed.

I spent the morning on the side porch studying until the phone rang. Mrs. McCutchan's voice on the line was calm but shaky. "Donna, William's been in an accident. He's okay. I've called the ambulance."

Adrenalin slammed through me. "Did he hit his head?"

"No." She paused. "A stick pierced his leg. But Robert, his friend, is a boy scout and helped him up the hill."

"I'll be right over." Never in my life have I felt so completely paralyzed. My heart pounded. My hands shook. My mind turned to mush. I prayed, "Lord take over now. Please." I took several deep breaths, threw on my coat and boots, frantically searched for my purse and keys, and miraculously made it to the garage and car.

Thanking the Lord that I had learned to drive on the snow-covered roads of Pennsylvania, I turned onto Petersburg Road right after the EMT unit. I felt relief at last, or so I thought, until he drove right past the McCutchan driveway. Flashing my lights and laying on the horn, I turned into the drive, ran into the house, and found William lying on his belly on the hardwood floor with Mrs. Mac holding four folded dishtowels over a wound on the back of his thigh.

I examined it. There was very little blood, but it was deep enough to need stitches. Of course, the ambulance EMTs stormed the house. They knelt beside him, took his vitals, and dressed the wound with gauze and tape. Dramatic William went into full swing chatter.

I looked at Mrs. McCutchan and said, "Thank you so much. You did everything perfectly."

Running her hand through her hair, she smiled. "Really, it was all Robert. He pulled the stick out and helped William walk up the hill to the house." I thanked Robert for his bravery.

Mrs. McCutchan had also called Mac, and she told me he was on his way. I rode in the ambulance with William. "Mommy," my son said, "how big is the hole in my leg?"

"Maybe about the size of a quarter but there is a possibility you will need some stitches." I told him. Ice storms followed by several inches of snow had made the roads treacherous. The ambulance crawled along with all the other traffic. William didn't cry or seem to be in any pain at all. He told me the whole story, and when he got to the part where the stick ripped his pants and poked a hole in his leg, I stopped him. "William. Did you get a look at the stick?"

"Why do you need know what the stick looked like?"

I tapped my finger on my head. "I was just thinking, you may need antibiotics. The condition of the stick may be valuable information for the doctors."

Excitedly, he piped up, "It was decaying!"

We were ushered into an ER room and the physician let me know that William needed stitches, as expected. The minute Mac showed up, my brave boy became a stranger's screaming child. The doctor looked at me and mouthed, "I've given him four times the usual numbing."

Nodding, I said, "No need to wait longer. Get it over. Stitch him up."

I bent to kiss the screaming demon and he stopped long enough to listen to me. I whispered, "I'm going to pediatrics to see if I can get you something. I'll be right back." His screams hit high notes I never knew were possible. I couldn't get out of there fast enough. There was a huge contrast between William with me and William with Mac. By the time I brought back a kiddie pack from pediatrics, William was dressed, walking about stiff legged, and milking his injury for every drop of attention.

Mac stopped by the pharmacy for William's antibiotics, dropped me off at his mother's to get my car, and then met me at the farm. We tucked William into bed that night and after he fell asleep, I had a major meltdown in front of Mac. "The only great thing that came out of our marriage came close to death today. If he had hit his head this night would have ended so differently."

Mac, being a rational man, said, "But he didn't hit his head. He just landed on a stick. A decaying stick at that." And he laughed so hard he almost fell on the icy driveway on the way to his car.

I waved good-bye at the door, smiled, and whispered "You just don't get me at all."

Chapter 29:

Mom, I Really Like This Guy. Can We Take Him Home?

others brag about their sons and daughters. William, my one and only son, amazed me at every stage of his life. Creativity lived in his bones and came out in drawing, playing piano, writing, and singing. He spread joy like honey on homemade biscuits. Because the McCutchans and I loved William, conflict between us never happened, until I met a nice guy.

In November of 1995 I attended a women's Christian retreat that a minister had recommended when I was still with Mac. He had adamantly refused to let me go. When an opportunity came for me to attend after the divorce, I took off a weekend and headed to Santa Claus, Indiana. I enjoyed three days filled with fun, music, and fifteen spiritual talks at a beautiful campground with thirty-five women plus a huge team of workers and spiritual directors.

My table leader let me read a sweet letter from her husband. Divorced women with children can develop an aversion to relationships. After more than five years of single-parenting, I happened to be content with school, work, and William. My stance did not go over well with several of the women, especially Doris. "Donna," she said, "I'll be praying for you a husband. Now when he shows up, I do have to meet him to be sure he is the right one." I hugged that sweet gray-haired woman good-bye on Sunday night and reluctantly promised to let her know if God answered her prayers.

On the way home from Santa Claus, I laid it out to God. "Lord, you know, I really don't want anyone. I'm not looking. If you think I need a man in my life, You'll have to make that happen, because I'm not hunting."

Faith retreats make lasting memories and friendships, but it's always good to get back home into routine. This retreat was called the Walk to Emmaus. The first thing William said to me when he got back from his dad's place was "Okay Mommy, and just how many miles did you walk?"

"Sorry, son. I didn't measure."

This retreat changed my life, especially when prayer warrior Doris hounded heaven for God to put a man in my life. The very Wednesday after the retreat I attended a Biomedical Ethics class in the huge auditorium on the USI campus. During a break my nurse friend Linda turned around and said "Hey girl, I found a friend who has a friend you need to meet. I hope it's okay. I gave her your number to give to him. Didn't think you'd mind. His name is Allen."

I chuckled to myself. Dagnabbit Doris, why so soon?

After class, I found out the details. I knew Linda's friend, Kathy. She had worked in the recovery room when I worked in the trauma unit years before. Allen and her husband went to school together and had maintained a close relationship through the years.

Allen did call me within the week, but I didn't like the dating scene. Previous relationships with some good men didn't pan out. I held unrealistic expectations for a soulmate, and I viewed myself as tarnished goods. I also knew I was not the easiest person to get along with. My European friend from church, AP, helped me understand myself. "Donna," he said, "You are the most intimidating woman I have ever met." Puzzled, I needed an explanation. "AP, what on earth do you mean by that?" Putting his arm around me, he said gently, "You're not needy." And that truth sank deep into my heart. "AP, you're right," I admitted. Wiping tears away, I said, "not by choice."

Allen and I kept our distance and talked for weeks on the phone before we ever met. Our first date was in late November; we went to Pizza Hut with William, my little date evaluator. We drove there in separate vehicles and met in the parking lot. After we were seated, placed our order, and shared small talk, Allen said, "Where are the restrooms? I want to wash my hands." Jumping out of the booth, William volunteered to serve as his guide. "Follow me. I'll take you." In seconds, William plopped back into his seat. "Mom, I really like this guy. Can we take him home?"

Allen turned out to be a hard-working heating and air conditioning man employed at another hospital system across town. Our late-night conversations revealed important commonalities. Allen loved God, gardening, his Brittany spaniel, and his family. He too had experienced a nasty divorce years earlier. He lived with one regret—no children of his own.

I softened restrictions and Allen came to the farm often. He loved my cooking, and a mutual bond with William happened naturally. It was going well. But just as I let my guard down and believed this match came directly from Doris and God, Allen slammed on the brakes right before Christmas.

After supper one night, a strange and serious look came over his face. Before clearing the table, he said, "I need to tell you something."

I leaned back in my chair and waited for a bomb to drop. And it did.

"When you came with me to the Wadesville church a woman I've dated off and on for several years saw us together," he said. "In the past, she played me like a yo-yo, dating me and a physician off and on." Looking down at his empty plate, Allen fiddled with his spoon. "Anyway, she wants me now and I am in love with her. I have to give her this chance or I'll always wonder."

I bolted out of my chair. "Well, then I guess you better go." Picking up the dirty dishes and silverware, I headed to the sink.

"Please let me help you do the dishes."

"Just go. I don't need your help. I don't need you." And Allen left.

Chapter 30:

The Russians Are Coming

oliday disappointments hurt no matter how well they're wrapped. I thought I'd be sharing Christmas of 1995 with Allen, but instead of mourning our time apart, I decided to spice up an elderly couple's day instead. I invited Bill and Rita, a couple from church, to my holiday feast.

Allen called and interrupted our meal. "Merry Christmas! I'd like to bring over some gifts for you and William if that's okay."

"I suppose." Part of me wanted to say no thanks, but instead I said, "William will be glad to see you. But I do have company."

"Oh. I won't stay long."

Feeling embarrassed, I said, "We didn't get you anything."

"I didn't expect you to. I do care about the two of you," he said kindly. "Thanks for letting me come by. I'll see you shortly."

The time was 4:00 p.m. when Allen arrived, and I had just started handing out pieces of pumpkin pie to my guests. I invited him to join us for dessert and coffee. William introduced Bill and Rita and then I asked Bill to tell the story of how we met.

"Well, after church I spied a car with a flat tire, so I waited to see if someone might need my help. The Toyota Celica belonged to Donna. I knew I had a bottle of fix-a-flat at home, so I ran home, got the stuff, and saved the day. Weeks later, she saved me."

I smiled at Bill and shook my head as I spooned homemade whipping cream onto my pumpkin pie. "Water aerobics is totally responsible for any help I gave you and Rita."

Allen set down his coffee. "Bill, help me out here. I'm totally confused. Donna saved you from what? Drowning? You don't do water aerobics, do you?" Bill threw back his head and laughed. "Donna, tell him the story."

I obliged. "During water aerobics at the university pool, another nurse informed me of a heartbreaking scenario. A patient cried unconsolably and convinced her husband to take her out of the nursing home. He did, against medical advice. Something made me call Bill that night."

Bill waved a hush signal and continued. "I felt like Rita was a POW in that place. She calmed down the minute we stepped inside our house. I'm not a nurse. I didn't know how to get Rita to swallow pills. A complete mystery to a WWII Navy veteran. Applesauce. She took them for Donna with applesauce."

Looking at Rita, I smiled, "You are a lucky lady." Unable to speak a word since her stroke, she reached over and took hold of Bill's hand and leaned her head on his arm.

Bill and Rita left before dark. I packed them a care package. After hugs of thanks, Allen and I walked them to their car. As we watched them drive away, Allen confessed. "When you said you had someone over, I thought it was another guy."

"That's funny. I really don't understand why you care."

Inside, we opened the gifts Allen had brought and enjoyed a few hours together with William. The evening ended on a bittersweet but kind note.

For the next few months, I enjoyed my life of work, church, friends, and William. Allen called from time to time, which irritated me. Why would he call me all the time when he was pursuing his girlfriend? He asked mutual friends about me all the time and every time they saw me, they told me. His mission to maintain our friendship aggravated and perplexed me.

Time passed. The fall of 1996 brought new and bizarre challenges. Mac called unexpectedly, interrupting my newest sewing project—making new cushions and a tablecloth for my wrought-iron chairs and table.

"Donna, I need to discuss something with you. Could you have supper with me at the Hornet's Nest? Mom can watch William."

"Sure." I straightened the upholstery fabric on my cutting table. "Is everything okay?"

After a long pause, he said, "I'll meet you there at 5:30 tonight."

Because the farm was five houses from the Hornet's Nest. Bill and I had become regulars of the quaint restaurant tavern back during remodeling days. We ordered cheese sticks and marinara and the Cod dinner. Mac drank his usual Long Island Iced Tea. Squishing my lemons into my water, I didn't waste any time. "Mac, what's going on?"

"I needed you to know my plans." He unzipped a black padded binder, opened it to a calendar, and grabbed his pen from an inside jacket pocket. I felt a business meeting approaching. "I joined a group from Kentucky, and we will be heading to Russia to meet women who are interested in coming to America to marry."

"Really, Mac? Have you lost your mind? You do know many of those women are gold diggers. You are kidding, right?"

Smirking with big eyes, he said, "Not kidding."

"You are going to Russia to buy a wife?" I wanted to squeeze my lemon right into his eyes.

"Find a woman and marry her. That's correct."

"Why Russia?"

"Russian women are more subservient."

At that I about choked on my water. "For heaven's sake," I said, dipping a cheese stick in the marinara, "you do remember I ironed your boxer shorts." I took a bite of cheese until it stretched out and fell on my chin. I quickly wiped my face.

The server brought our meal and while we ate, Mac raved on about his marvelous future life with a Russian wife. I wondered what became of the consistently organized, frugal banker. The man across the booth from me looked like Mac, his voice sounded like Mac, but honestly, this irrational plan—there was no way that came from the Mac I used to know. I kept waiting for him to chuckle out a "Gotcha. Just kidding." But he didn't.

Mac ordered after-dinner coffee with Kahlua, which surprised me. I thought he was done with the meeting. Mac looked sheepish. "Well, I wanted to give you a heads up. No surprises, you know. Um." He took a drink of his coffee and closed his eyes and quickly said, "You have to move out of the farm. Not right away, but soon. This process takes months and several trips to Russia."

"Okay." This was the final blow. "Mac, I knew this day would come. I can't live there forever, nor can I afford to buy you out. Have you considered what William will think about all this? Or have you told him?"

"Not yet, but I will at the right time."

After we said our goodbyes, sadness overcame me when I turned up the paved drive to the farmhouse. My woods, my five acres, my flower beds, my clothesline, my vegetable garden, my home—not mine yesterday, today, or tomorrow.

There was no time to mourn the loss of things that never belonged to me. Besides, the Russians were coming, and I jumped into high gear.

Chapter 31:

Cold Feet

I 'd rather clean my ceiling fans than go house hunting. There's nothing like stepping over piles of dirty clothes and underwear peeled, dropped, or flung on bedposts or chairs. Armies of Cheerios marched along baseboards. One three car garage was gingerly opened by a realtor, who warned me to "Please stand back several feet." The boxes stacked from floor to ceiling inside swayed in the wind. The house was no better. A narrow path twisted and turned to and through every room. The one advantage of house hunting was that it drove me to clean and throw out gobs of stuff when I got home.

Assessing structures, foundations, roofing, and plumbing required a knowledgeable man. I phoned a friend. "Allen," the phone only rang once when he answered. "You must have been sitting on the phone."

"I have caller ID. It's great to hear from you. What's up?"

"As long as it's okay with your girlfriend, do you mind looking at a house with me and William on Friday night? I'll fix you supper."

"Sounds good to me."

Peace came with access to Allen's critical mind and questioning insight. He not only knew heating and air conditioning systems, but also had worked for years in construction. The next night we met and checked out a house for sale by owner. After meeting the owners and their two little children, Allen and I got permission to examine the heating and air conditioning system in the basement. Allen said, "This is one old furnace that needs to be replaced. Did you notice the little kids and parents wearing wool socks, slippers, and down vests? Bet they have cold feet."

We took their information, thanked them for their time, and went home to scalloped potatoes and ham, coleslaw, mixed vegetables, and homemade apple dumplings. One thing I knew about Allen's girlfriend—he told me once that she never cooked for him. After William went to bed, Allen and I sat in front of the fire and talked. "Are you and your girl getting along?"

Putting another log on the fire, he smiled. "I don't have a girlfriend."

"What? What happened?"

He shrugged and said, "I threw her in the trash."

"Allen Dale, what did you do?"

"I guess you spoiled me. I want to be with you and William."

Smirking, I said, "Do you want to know what I think?" And before Allen had a chance to answer, I blurted, "You got hungry. You missed my cooking."

"That too." He stoked the fire with the poker. "At least I know a good thing when I see it." He told me how much he had missed me and William. He said, "I know without any doubt, she is not for me. Why do you think I kept calling you?"

I shook my head "Do you have any idea how much it hurt when you left me? It will take me some time."

"I get it. Those kids aren't the only ones with cold feet." Allen stood in front of the fire warming his hands. "I can wait. You'll see."

"Sure."

We kept house hunting together on my days off. I wish we had kept a journal in those days. Jokes flew. Allen loved a flat yard, and if we found a nice house with a steep incline, he'd swing a hand at an incline and say, "Nah, too much slope. You'd have to tie a rope to the mower. Not doing it." We saw gorgeous homes with no lawn and horrible homes with acres. Allen spied foundation cracks and water issues. When one homeowner asked us to take off our shoes, we obliged. After walking on the basement carpet, we left with sopping socks. Thumbs down.

One cute home had a downstairs that had been converted into a lovely all-purpose room, a potential man cave. The sellers were short. Allen is six feet tall, and his hair brushed the ceiling. "Allen, if we buy that house, Gary can't ever go into basement." Allen's brother Gary was six-foot-four. "He'd push up the ceiling tiles."

Our relationship not only healed with time but grew. When things got serious, we made an appointment to see Freddie. He counseled us, administered a compatibility test, and reviewed the favorable results. I felt so good. The test showed strong commonalities with few negative warning signs.

In October of 1996 Allen popped the question while we sat on a bench in the middle of the mall. We picked out my engagement ring together. I was happy. Life moved in the right direction at a healthy pace. Everything fell into place for Allen, me, and William. Finally, we bought our house beautiful, the Pink Palace.

The house met most of my requirements—perfect middle school and high school district, the perfect commute for Allen and me, perfect mature trees, and a perfect non-sloped yard. Proud as peacocks, we started work immediately on the landscape and gardens, knowing the interior needed a major overhaul. The previous owner, an interior decorator, believed pink was the color of calm. I stood amazed that wall to wall carpet came in Pepto-Bismol pink. The cream baseboards provided only temporary relief as pink, green, and white striped wallpaper flew up the wall to the chair rail, where it met a border full of pink peacock couples looking into each other's eyes. We agreed to set major interior renovations on hold until after our wedding, which we planned for April 12, 1997. We adjusted to the pink interior and to our soon-to-be-blended family. Mac never did.

Mac got drunk too often. Uncertainty and fear gripped me every time Mac's visitation time with William came around. During drop off, I conducted a surreptitious Clinical Institute Withdrawal Assessment, a protocol for determining alcohol withdrawal; Mac never knew, and he failed it often during those days.

One day I brought Mac to the house and made him bean soup and a hamburger. He hadn't eaten in days. I'll never forget William leaning against the doorframe, staring at his dad from the kitchen. Mac sat on the recliner in the living room, talking at him with slurred speech, attempting to make a point with a powerless arm and finger. His eyes were blood-shot, and his head kept bobbing forward to his chest and then back into the recliner pillow. "Mac," I said, covering him up with a throw while he adjusted the recliner, "just sleep a bit. I'll have your lunch ready soon."

I believe that day revealed a sad reality to both William and me. Mac was a true alcoholic, living in an addictive despair, while our life sailed on.

William loved the Titanic, and he helped us pick the date of our wedding. Honestly, I can never remember if he chose the day the unsinkable ship hit the iceberg or the day it finally capsized. Regardless, our wedding was lovely. The three of us sang "Household of Faith" after lighting the unity candle, along with our tenor friend, Dave Pugh. We forgot to set out tissues in the pews. Our song touched everyone.

Usually the early months of marriage promise excitement, adventure, and uncertainty. Allen and I experienced those things, not because we were settling into a life of peaceful love and contentment, but because of my ex-husband's climb up the alcoholic ladder of harassment. We took drastic measures— we took out a restraining order on Mac, and life got ugly. It got really ugly.

Chapter 32:

The Year of the Boozer

M ac tried to jump off the alcoholic train alone, a task that has proved to be Mission Impossible for so many. Mac lost his job. His mother paid his bills, either oblivious to the magnitude of his addiction or simply in denial.

In the summer of 1998, he promised to be sober and set up a vacation to take William to California. I noticed his stagger the moment I got out of the car to drop William off. Mac had moved to the farm once we moved out. His Russian love was still in Russia.

"Hey, William, go jump on the trampoline while I talk with your dad." I said, and then I turned to my ex-husband. "Okay, Mac let's walk around the gardens." I took hold of his arm to steady his gait as he scuffled along. "Mac, you're drunk. What were you thinking? Let's go into the house and dump your stash."

"You, oh you rotten woman."

"Come on Mac, let me try to help you."

He agreed, and we walked into the kitchen. He reached into a high cabinet and grabbed a half-full bottle of Vodka. Turning on the water in the sink, I said, "Give me that."

He removed the lid with shaking hand and quickly turned the bottle up and poured it down his throat. I could not believe it.

"That's it Mac. I am so done." I bolted down the side porch and opened the door to go, but before I stepped out the door an angry hand clamped down on my arm. His warm alcoholic breath fell on my neck with every slurry word. "Oh no, no, no, you don't."

"Mac, you are such a wonderful man." I knew stroking his ego to be my only hope. "You love William so much. You can take William on another vacation once you've kicked this drinking. You can do it." I gently pried his fingers from my forearm. "I have faith in you, Mac. I know you won't let us down."

The minute I broke away I yelled to William. "Run, William, run fast. Get into the car. We need to get out of here now." William jumped off the trampoline and listened without question. I drove straight to the sheriff's office and got a restraining order.

I called Allen and let him know what happened. When I got home, we devised a plan for me to take William on a vacation out of town. I called work and easily got time off. To reduce dad disappointment, I suggested we drive through Ohio to Pennsylvania and hit all the antique shops. It wasn't as attractive as a trip to California, but I knew my twelve-year-old William loved antiquing. Allen agreed to stay home and hold down the fort. Neither of us were prepared for what drunken Mac might try.

The fastest vacation planning and packing in my lifetime happened that day. The phone rang incessantly. We never answered. I told Allen not to tell Mac anything. I also said, "Just don't answer the phone." Incessant ringing drove Allen nuts. He answered the phone to a subdued and soft-spoken Mac.

"Allen, can I talk to Donna?"

"Mac, she's not here."

"Oh man. Can I talk to William?"

"They've gone."

"Can you help me, Allen? Can you come take me to rehab?"

Of course, Allen called me and relayed the entire story. He went to the farm to pick up Mac and helped him pack a bag. On the top of the dresser sat a .38 revolver. Mac saw Allen looking at the gun and said, "Today has been a dark day for me."

Allen drove Mac directly to the rehab only to find out that admission after hours required a physician evaluation. Allen took Mac to his workplace, the Baptist hospital emergency room. Mac paced about the waiting room like a hungry caged animal. Obnoxious loud cussing flowing freely from his mouth. Allen tried to calm him down to no avail and ushered him outside to wait by the glass doors. Finally, the staff waved at Allen and called Mac back to a room.

The staff pressed him hard. "Why should we believe you will stay and complete the program?" The psychiatric evaluator reviewed his past records. A couple months before this night, Allen and I had convinced Mac to get into the in-patient rehab. When he was asked about failed relationships Mac checked himself out. The staff informed Mac, "You can't just jump in and out of our program. We need to re-evaluate you."

Still pacing angrily, Mac said "Enough of this. Take me home, Allen." And Allen did.

William and I returned from our vacation, safe and happy. Of course, Mac constantly called, begging us to remove the restraining order. The embarrassment seemed sure to kill him. We agreed to discuss it to ensure his presence at a meeting with all our attorneys. Everyone, including his attorneys, knew our good intentions. The joint custody agreement was changed, depending on his completion of an alcoholic rehab program. We all pleaded with him to get help, even as an outpatient. Instead of pursuing rehab, he pursued his Russian solution.

Off to Russia he went. He called Allen and me daily to ask our opinion of which woman he should choose. Mac's wife lottery came down to a young, athletic 24-year-old or an educated 33-year-old English teacher with a little girl. What a privilege to help a drunken millionaire decide on such an asset, a bride.

I feared more for his life than his choice. William's dad staggered through the streets of Russia, calling and telling us stories of being in bars filled with rough-looking men who glared at him with red devil eyes. Mac, afraid, made us even more worried. We prayed for him, and eventually he came home safely with a new family. Mac agreed with our suggestion to choose the English teacher with the four-year-old daughter. Even William got excited at having a little stepsister. I hoped his future stepmother possessed kind mothering skills.

Not long after they settled in at the farm, we invited them over. We welcomed them with open arms, and I honestly wanted a healthy blended family. I hoped for too much.

Tatyana met me with dark, disdain-filled eyes. She hung all over Mac like a teenager. The little girl didn't speak English. She resembled a four-year-old, black-haired Shirley Temple. Her name was Luba, which means "love" in Russian, and we loved her instantly.

Trips back and forth to the farm to pick up and deliver William from activities brought multiple interesting encounters. One day, I walked the gardens with little Luba and shared a packet of Graham crackers with her. She ran up to her mother and shot out an excited bunch of Russian words. Tatyana glared at me and translated. "Luba says, she wishes you were her mother."

That was definitely a disastrous moment in my Dale Carnegie effort to win friends and influence Mac's new family. Despite how hard Allen, William, and I tried, things progressed from bad to worse. Mac kept drinking, and once he knocked his mother down, intentionally or unintentionally, in front of Tatyana. Pre-nuptial agreement or no pre-nuptial agreement, she witnessed that and threatened to leave him.

William, Allen, and I talked honestly with Mac about the situation. Tatyana despised me and Mac knew it. He told me it was a cultural thing.

"All Russian women hate the ex-wives." William didn't have good feelings about her either, especially after she ran over his dog with the jeep when she was learning to drive. She screamed Russian phrases, threw up her hands, and peeled out down the drive while engaging in a hysterical fit. She left William to scrape up our faithful beagle mix Tag and bury him in the garden.

Even after that demonstration of insensitivity, the three of us came to a decision. They deserved a chance, especially Luba. Besides, if they went back to Russia, Mac might replace Tatyana with someone worse.

Persuasion tactics worked for all. We convinced Mac to save his new family. The Russian promised to stay only if he got help. For the first time, he committed to doing that. He had refused to get sober for his mom, his dad, or his son, but for Miss Subservient he gave it all. He signed up to an outpatient program with our full support and prayers, and after several months he came out clean, dry, and mean.

Chapter 33:

Tears, Floods, & Food

I believe most people who remarry try hard to create a sensitive transition for their children. I guess I'm naïve. Mac and his bride didn't fall into the category of "most people." Mac's new Russian family stole all of his affection, attention, and allegiance. Somehow during this Russian invasion, Mac forgot his one and only son, William.

I knew William suffered, but I never knew how much until he crafted a poem the day after his thirteenth birthday.

Sadness
Smells like dead flowers.
Tastes like bad food.
Sounds like a little kid crying.
Feels like someone constantly breaking their promises.
Looks like a house that has burnt to the ground.

William A. McCutchan
1-13-99

This broke my heart. My son, my one and only son, expressed a pain that was deep and raw and much too familiar. A promise from my teenage years haunted me. The one thing I had never wanted for my children when I dreamt of motherhood was a life of broken promises. I agonized as I wondered why William and I shared parallel childhood lives. I guess any family can foster dysfunction. Children deal with it in their own way. Anger tried to sprout in William's tender heart. Allen and I usually tried creative ways to change negative behaviors.

One memorable event happened at suppertime. Allen and William sat at the kitchen bar while I filled their plates with tender beef, green beans, whipped potatoes, and gravy. When a hateful, hurtful comment flew out of William's mouth, I lost total control of my arm. Whap. Warm mashed potatoes missed the plate and plopped on the top of William's head.

"Oh Mom," William said, tentatively touching the taters, "I can't believe you did that."

Allen's eyes screamed with horror as I read his mind. I knew he lamented the loss of his second helping. Somehow the homemade version of Mr. Potato Head lightened William's life with laughter. And we laughed a lot. I provided much of the material.

The night I jumped on the piano bench screaming while a mouse and her babies scrambled across the hard wood floor, William doubled over red-faced. "Mother it's just a little mouse family." Allen and the dog took care of the mice and William helped calm me down.

Brittany, Allen's old Brittany spaniel, loved William. When Allen lived alone, he never let his dog out of the kitchen. She slept on a tiny rug. When she moved in with us, all restrictions were lifted. Like a queen, Brittany slept in William's bed or laid on the couch with her head in his lap. No matter what a day brings, a wagging butt and tail from a cream and roan Brittany helps. So do friends.

Our church family meant a lot to us all. When we first bought the house, Allen and I took a Discipleship class with a great group of friends at the church. I'll never forget the look on the minister's face when I made an announcement. "You're all invited to our new house. We're having a stripping party." Looking at the gang I felt my face turn beet red. "Oh guys," shaking my head, "not that kind of stripping. We're stripping wallpaper."

They all showed up, sprayed glue remover, chiseled down the pink peacocks, and stuffed them in trash bags with grace. Some churches live their love. Mine does. The following Easter, in pouring down rain, they came not to strip wallpaper but to shovel sand.

Pastor Doug gave a fantastic Easter message that year. The takeaway: when you need help, call someone. We did. Flood waters rise fast in Evansville, and our house sat in the flood zone. The county graciously dumped a huge load of sand in the driveway, along with bags. My friends instantly turned into professional sandbag makers.

Crying, I looked at the pastor through the rain and said, "Doug, you can't say we didn't listen to your message. We needed help, we called, and Blue Grass Church came to the rescue."

Years later a hundred-year flood hit. Tragically, the city and county ran out of sand. They brought us a meager pile of it and some empty bags at noon. I was home alone, and I dreaded the prospect of facing the onslaught of water without any sandbags. I called William and Allen (who worked until 4:00) to let them change their route home. Our street flooded fast.

I had just hung up the phone from talking to Allen when the doorbell rang. Two strapping guys with shovels stood there smiling. "Hi. Are you William's mom? He called us to help make sandbags." I said, "I've never been so glad to see anyone." The three of us had all the sandbags made and placed. Our efforts looked like we tried to make a levee with toothpicks as the water crept up the driveway.

The next day I went to work. I taught ten nursing students clinicals at a nursing home for the University of Southern Indiana. Early that morning I called the department head for this course to let them know about my situation. "My house is in the flood zone and when the county delivers a load of sand, I need to go. I'll give students an alternative assignment."

By mid-morning, I received a call from my neighbor to let me know that the sandman had come. I explained the situation to the students, and then something amazing happened. Five asked if they could come to help as a community service project. These young women and men from a variety of cities worked tirelessly to help make sandbags for me and for my neighbors. I witnessed caring on steroids from future nurses.

That same afternoon, my church family once more showed up and like true family, they set up tables, jumped into the kitchen, and put out a spread of food for the entire neighborhood and all of the workers. Our home and garage were dry. Our electricity and water were safe and working. Our home became Food Central during floods, holidays, and musicals.

For Christmas break gatherings during William's high school years, I fixed soups, sandwiches, relish, hot chocolate, and desserts. We invited neighborhood teens to meet at our house and then go caroling. Usually only a group of girls showed up, although guys were invited.

A funny thing happened while we sang our way up and down the hills of our subdivision. Every time we caroled at one of the guys' houses and they found out we had supper waiting, they grabbed their coats and joined the group. After an hour of singing, teens piled into our house. I loved taking in the scenes of guys and girls chowing down at the table, playing piano, and enjoying the fire in the family room. Our home's arms stayed open for William and his friends all his life. His friends were my friends too.

One day I was home alone, knitting a scarf in front of the fireplace, when someone knocked on the glass sliding doors of our screened-in porch. A group of girls had found a lost dog with tags and wanted to use my phone. Stamping the snow off their boots, they piled into the family room and warmed their hands by the fire. One of the girls called the owner. The address in hand, they were getting ready to take the golden retriever home when one of the girls said, "What are you making?"

"A scarf," I told her.

"Man, I would love to know how to knit." The blonde with the big blue eyes tilted her head and watched me intently. "Could you teach us? Could we come back?"

Thus, my precious group of teenage Knitterenas came back and spent the entire afternoon learning to knit. I gave each girl a set of needles and a skein of yarn, and they quickly grasped the basic purl and knit stitches. A week later, one of the girls called and asked a favor. "I messed up a couple rows on my scarf and I don't know how to fix it. I'm heading to the mall. If I drop off my scarf, can you fix it for me and then I'll pick it up on my way home?"

"Of course." I fixed her mistake and worked several rows. Being available to help William's friends made me happy. I loved to feed them too.

William sang in the choir during high school, and when he was a junior, he shared the lead of Ravenal in *Showboat*. We lived close to the school and during rehearsal nights, William called religiously. "Hey Mom, what's for supper, and how many can I bring?"

At every rehearsal supper we fed a different group of teenagers. I will never forget the night I tried a new recipe of meatball sandwiches on crunchy hoagie buns. I thought soup, salad, and sandwiches would be nourishing and filling. I calculated wrong. I ran out of meatballs.

"Okay, does anyone want tuna salad sandwiches?" I was unprepared for the response. Five hands flew up in the air.

"I love tuna!"

"I want one too!"

"Can you put lettuce and tomato on mine?"

I considered these kids Olympians camouflaged as singers. They licked the platter and our cupboard clean. When the gang left for rehearsal, Allen and I gave thanks to God for our peanut butter and jelly sandwiches and glasses of milk.

Somehow the reputation of the Kincheloe kitchen reached the ears of the musical director. She called me one morning and volunteered Allen and I to pull together a meal for the cast prior to the last performance. I'm not a caterer. Feeding six or eight kids supper was easy, but the thought of feeding over eighty-five cast members scared me. I reached out to great church friends, excellent cooks with kids in the musical, and together we put out quite a spread.

The gratitude of those weary, talented teenagers far outweighed any work or cost on our behalf. This time of serving and supporting these young people, along with my dear friends, was the very definition of loving acts worth remembering.

Allen and I lived to do just that for William. Powerless to remove sadness, we let love power our actions. This is, I believe, the secret recipe for making memories that bring children back for more.

Chapter 34:

Character and Accountability

M y father used to say, "You can tell the character of a man by the way he treats his mother." I prefer to paraphrase this saying by exchanging the word "mother" with "grandmother." William spent every weekend during his senior year in high school caring for his confused Nana along with the twenty-four-hour nurse aides. He watched her mind deteriorate. Mrs. McCutchan knew it, too. The saddest part of her dementia is that Mrs. McCutchan knew her loss and often said, "William, I am so befuddled."

William hosted parties with his friends and played his grandmother her favorite songs on the player piano. His character shined. His beloved Nana passed in June of 2004. That day Tatyana exposed her true character.

William told me he received his marching orders from Tatyana while he sat in Mrs. McCutchan's living room on the day of the funeral. "William," she told him in her thickly Russian-accented English, "you are no longer welcome in this house." Is it possible to double break a human heart? Burying Nana and then, just hours later, being banished was a hard way to lose a home that occupied a huge chunk of William's precious childhood memories. Mac agreed to Tatyana's conniving, but he did allow William to live at the farm with some friends.

During this time William worked crazy retail hours at a popular store at the mall. During his free time, he worked diligently towards his dream of becoming an architect. From the time William could hold a pencil, he had always loved to draw houses. He remodeled the garages at the farm with a friend and submitted this project to Ball State University's Architecture program. Despite Mac's negativity when William told him about it—"Architects starve," he said—William ignored his dad, pursued his dream, got accepted, and moved on with his life. The first year he lived on campus his grades and energy took off. Mac's life took off too, in a different direction—downward.

Mac's perfect subservient beauty strayed. Tatyana engaged in an affair, and she and Mac got the quickest divorce ever. Mac kept the prenuptial agreement, dished out $10,000, and Tatyana was gone. Regardless of the contention the Russians brought into William's life, Allen and I felt sorry for Mac. Dealing with the stress of abandonment and loss of dreams, no matter how bizarre they may be, is difficult. With the addition of a prostate cancer diagnosis to that emotional insult we watched a controlling man transform into a crushed, crippled soul.

When the diagnosis hit, Mac turned leech-like. He demanded Will come home every weekend. He obsessed about getting his house in order. He fine-tuned his will and delivered a sealed copy to me. He refused the curative treatment and opted for chemo, radiation, or anything possible to stay alive.

Such a diagnosis might have provided rationale for an alcoholic to reach for vodka, but Mac did not. He took another road. He chose to visit the gambling boat docked by the waterfront. I gave him a twenty-dollar bill once and he returned to our house with a thousand dollars. I always wondered if he really won it or grabbed it out of his safe.

He called and dropped by often during those days. I think he was lonely. He shared jokes with Allen, and they fostered a kind relationship with each other. He surprised us by sharing some of his ammunition stash. Mac, a doomsday prepper, built a safe room and stuffed shelves with alcohol for trading purposes, paper goods, rations, and water. The heavy fireproof safe held coins, guns, and ammo. He paid contractors to build him a concrete block section in the basement. In private, Allen and I snickered at that. He had built this when his Russian family lived with him, yet only one folding lawn chair fit inside the safety chamber.

Living alone is hard for a lot of people. Living alone in a huge, empty house where both your father and mother died is creepy. Lucky for Mac, his house didn't stay empty. Tatyana's affair did not pan out. She begged for forgiveness, and Mac took her and Luba back with open arms and an open wallet. She vowed to take care of him through his cancer journey. At some point in this soap opera, they also moved Tatyana's mother in from Russia. That drama played out without additional input from William, Allen, and me, thank God!

During William's college years, from 2005–2009, our life was full. Allen and I worked at the hospitals, served on multiple Christian retreats, taught Sunday school, gardened, and remodeled our home. The best part of those years was filled with friends and several vacations linked to writing conferences.

I wanted to be a writer. That desire is strange to confess, for in a way it is like a curse, an elusive dream, a nagging force that pushes and pulls. The craft of writing is not a gift from birth. The necessities of the writing life are education, writing, and for me, accountability partners. Allen and I made plans to go to Colorado for a writer's conference with the intent to present my Sunday school lessons to editors.

Months before the trip, I invited my friends Cheryl and her husband Jon to help me organize my lessons. Cheryl worked in a physician's office and had organizational skills I lacked. Jon, a Navy veteran and healthcare worker in an ambulatory surgical office, added a man's perspective. Both brought a deep Bible knowledge and love for God. They understood my motive for sharing sound educational messages. Making money took a back seat to touching lives with hope.

I filled up a six-foot table with several months' worth of middle school games and lessons. During one of our discussions, Cheryl picked up a stack of papers and said, "Donna, what's this?"

I quickly flipped through the pages, "Oh Cheryl, those stories from patients and families are for a book I'm going to write someday." Before I could put the stack of mismatched papers back in some semblance of order, Jon said, "Donna, may I see those?" I handed them over, and he began to read. The three of us began to cry. Cheryl shook her pointer at me. "This book is more important," she said, waving her arms over the piles of lessons, "than all of this."

Accountability did it for me. Jon and Cheryl came for supper every few weeks and we sifted over chapters, typed, reviewed, scrutinized scripture passages, and prayed. Always, we prayed.

The experience of a mega-conference is unforgettable. The people and the God connections amazed me. No, I did not get an editor. I got depressed and discouraged. I was fit to quit until Tammy called to find out about my trip. She had generously given me the story of the death of Colin, her little boy. When she found out I wanted to forget publishing all together, her comment pierced me. "Donna, Colin needs to preach. You know he always wanted to be a preacher like his grandpa, and your book will be his only chance. You cannot stop now." So, I listened. When other people give you the privilege of writing their stories, the book belongs to everyone mentioned. I self-published, packaged and sold over 3000 books. Colin got to preach, as did the others whose stories I shared.

Some goals in life sit on a shelf, hidden from view. Accountability partners will hunt down the goal, dust it off, throw it to you, and expect follow-through. Be thankful for them!

Chapter 35:

Nursing Family

Nurses care for strangers who become family at the hospital—an expectation of the profession. Nursing one's own family members stretches, strains, cements, or breaks healthy or sick relationships. Nurses calmly accept personal family dynamic challenges. But when an ex-husband prefers care from his ex-wife and son over his newest wife and daughter, craziness jumps on everyone. And man did it jump!

One day in May 2012, Will called me on my cell phone, worried, after he and his friend checked on Mac at the McCutchan mansion. "Mom. Something is bad wrong with Dad." His, heavy syncopated sigh gave me pause.

"Will, hold on a minute, I need to pull over." I stopped in a parking lot. "Okay Will, what's going on??

"Mom, he's talking out of his head and he can barely walk."

"Will, he needs to go to the hospital now. Do you need me to help you?"

"No. My friend and I can get him in the car. Dad wants you. Can you come?"

"Of course." I felt strange about the potential situation. "Where on earth are the Russians?"

Will snickered. "Huh. She's on vacation in Florida celebrating Luba's sixteenth birthday."

Within an hour Will texted me the room number. By the time I arrived, labs, X-rays, and CT scans had been completed. Mac's sodium level had hit extreme lows, which is what had caused his confusion. Saline IVs and salt tablets helped clear his mind.

I sat in the chair beside Mac and the three of us did not talk much. Weak and weary, Mac held onto his cell phone in case Tatyana called. Will had contacted her at Mac's request. Will never sat idle well, especially in a hospital. He folded Mac's clothes perfectly, a skill acquired from working in retail, and put everything in the closet.

Mac started giving us instructions in an uncharacteristically kind voice. "Will, get the ring of keys out of my pants pocket." Pointing at me, he said, "Go with William to my office in the basement and get my living will, the advanced directive for the hospital record, from the tall, locked filing cabinet."

Will and I set off on our mission to a house neither of us had entered in years. It's funny to think how a person names a house. Will called this house "Nana's." Even though his dad and Tatyana, Luba, and Tatyana's mother lived there, the name never changed for him. I also had a name for that house. I had called it the McCutchan mansion for years. Lately, I renamed it the death house. Will's grandparents had both died in that house. Mac planned to do the same.

While Will played roulette with the file cabinet keys, I played snoop. Mac, a proud banker, had always kept his desk organized and bare, but it certainly wasn't bare anymore. Shocked, I said, "Will, your dad is in worse shape than we ever imagined." William looked as I waved the three-inch stack of overdue and unpaid bills and shook his head.

Frustrated after trying key after key, Will yelped. "Finally, found the right one." He proceeded to finger through the tightly packed folders in search of the living will. Pulling out a handful of folders, Will walked over to the basement kitchenette and tossed them on the counter by the printer. "Well, here's something I want to read," he remarked.

"What did you find?"

Smiling like the Cheshire Cat, he said, "The newest prenuptial agreement."

When Tatyana's affair did not pan out the way she had hoped it would, she called Mac. He took her back. They lived together unmarried for some time. When Mac received his terminal diagnosis, he remarried Tatyana. Like most Christian believers, he feared hell, and he believed living with a woman outside of marriage to be an unforgivable sin.

In Will's eyes the remarriage caused severe pain. Unkindness and conflict can burn.

The copy machine on the counter hummed as we copied anything Will wanted. We locked up the office and returned to the hospital.

Mac gave approval for me to have access to all test results and to discuss his case with his care team. I had worked in this hospital for years and knew the physicians and nurses well. Results came in and outcomes were poor. Despite radiation beads and multiple chemo treatments, cancer lit up throughout his body.

Gingerly, I brought up the bill situation. "Mac, I couldn't help but notice you have a huge stack of bills on your desk."

"Yeah. You and Will get those bills and pay them together. William, your name is on all my accounts."

"Gee, Mac," I hesitated, "What about Tatyana?"

He wrinkled his nose, "She doesn't access my accounts. She only has credit cards." Winking at Will, Mac said, "I know your mother knows how to balance a checkbook, like me. I taught her myself, years ago."

And what an eye-opening, jaw-dropping experience that was, to see the life of a subservient spender detailed down to the last penny. Days later, Will and I sat at a table in the garage of the new house Allen and I had purchased—we took possession the very day Mac fell ill—and got to work.

Balancing someone else's neglected checkbook without controlling spending is more than impossible—it smacks you upside the head with insanity. Digging through his account records like criminal investigators, Will and I discovered that Mac's loving wife spent between $6,000 to $8,000 per month. Over their married, divorced, and remarried life of twelve years, she had easily gone through at least $1 million, maybe more.

Will wrote check after check as I addressed and stamped the envelopes. We created our own documentation system using composition books. I prayed the shopping flings might stop soon, for balance of the outgo always ended with little fluff left in the balance column. This put me on edge as I watched Will stand by while Tatyana whittled away at Mac's financial legacy.

To add to this, the sound of broken glass smashing on concrete pulled Will and me out of our bill funk. From our garage we often enjoyed watching the scenes of spring activity by the next-door neighbors. The white-haired woman whipped electric trimmers over the boxwoods at the front of her house while an elderly man cleaned out the shed in the middle of the backyard. The whirl of the trimmer stopped quickly with the crashing glass. Cries for help floated into the garage. "Richard, Richard, I need help."

The slightly slouched elderly man stepped out of the shed, turned, and headed to the front of the house. Immediately I recognized the Parkinson's shuffle, an inch-by-inch stride. So did Will.

Will's eyes grew large. "Mom, I think we better go help. If that guy is Richard, she'll be lucky if he gets there by dark." We threw the bills and papers in our bill box and ran next door. Broken glass from the storm door had sliced the woman's arm. I grabbed a white towel off a set of golf clubs leaning against the brick house, wrapped the wound and held tight pressure.

The injured woman (who we learned was named Darlene) smiled and said, "What a fine way to meet new neighbors. Somehow, I lost my balance with the trimmer and fell through the glass storm door." We called 911. Richard finally showed up. He came through the back door and started to pick the glass shards out of the door. Will stopped him quickly. Another neighbor, Sharon, came to help.

After the ambulance carried Darlene and Richard to the hospital, Will, Sharon, and I picked up the glass. Will dragged our garden hose over to wash the blood off the front stoop. We gathered up the shrub trimmings from the front flower bed.

As we walked back over to our garage, I put my arm around William's shoulders. "Son, thanks so much for helping me."

"Mom, no matter where we are, we are always the ones helping everyone else."

I agreed. "We make a good team, Will. I'm so glad you're mine. Always."

Chapter 36:

Glide or Dive

S ome years glide along like a kite riding the wind perfectly, even landing without damage. Some years the string breaks or it gets tangled in a tree for life. The year 2013 was more like a dive than a glide.

Cancer continued to ravage Mac, bouncing him in and out of the hospital multiple times. Like a needle stuck on an old LP, he wanted Will and me to help him every time. One admission landed Mac in the Neuro ICU. A limp right arm and leg and slurred incomprehensible speech screamed stroke. A Mensa member, whose brain held a monstrous vocabulary, was reduced to helpless frustration by his inability to stack a noun or verb in any semblance of sentence structure. The only time Mac spoke he swore.

Walking with me down to the elevators after visiting hours Will said, "Mom, of all the words in Dad's head, why are swear words the only ones he remembers?"

At twenty-six, Will's medical knowledge seemed equivalent to several nursing courses in critical care. I realized that stroke education had never been needed until now. I said, "People with brain cancer or traumatic brain injury often experience verbal aggression. If this is a stroke, it can improve once the swelling goes down."

"Knowing Dad, he's probably cussing on purpose."

Over time, Mac did improve. Will, Allen, and I came to see him in the hospital. If Tatyana happened to be there when we showed up, she grabbed up her purse, kissed Mac on the forehead and left. Will and I knew her favorite parting words. "I must go. I must go."

Not everyone is capable of caregiving. Tatyana got pale and weak and even passed out on the floor during one of Mac's ICU encounters. When Mac ended up with a tracheostomy and a nighttime home ventilator, this seemed too much for Tatyana.

A motley crew attended educational sessions on caring for his trach and vent prior to his discharge home. Allen, Will, Charlie (Mac's handyman and friend), I, and of course Tatyana needed to become familiar with the alarm systems and the proper settings.

Tatyana was distracted and disinterested, and the minute the session engaged in hands-on practice, she flew out the door like a hawk, screeching, "I must go. I must go." All of us thought she might be on the hunt again.

The closer Mac's discharge came, the more his wife leaned on Will and me. Tatyana was scared to death of bringing Mac home from the specialty hospital with his trach and respirator. I offered to deliver him. When we arrived at the McCutchan mansion, he bounded out of the car. Once I caught up with him, I reached out to help him up the steps to the door. Mac slapped my hand and scowled, "I'm doing this on my own power. Leave me alone. You can go now."

As a patient in my work environment, Mac wanted my knowledge, relationships, and help. The minute his feet touched McCutchan soil, however, an ugly spirit of superiority sprouted up in him to put me in my place. I watched him struggle up the stairs and then left, hoping his family was home.

When he wasn't called upon to take care of his father, Will loved his job working at an auctioneering company. He drove about an hour back and forth to work and put in some long days. His new routine included being awakened all through the night by his father's text messages while three Russian women slept soundly in their upstairs bedrooms.

When Tatyana and Mac shared the big downstairs bedroom, she moved a double bed into the room under the bay window. Mac slept in the king bed and she slept in the double. His snoring could wake the dead. As Mac's health deteriorated, Tatyana loosened restrictions on Will and invited him to sleep over with his dad. What a reversal! She shifted suddenly from "you're not welcome" to "please come anytime, sleep over, take care of your father, and you can even have a key."

Finally, they hired a homecare company and girls came and stayed the night. If the agency girls cancelled, Tatyana called Will. If Mac needed his trach suctioned, Tatyana called Will. If he needed a shot, Tatyana called Will. Will always came.

In the fall of 2013, months of juggling work and nursing his dad finally caught up with Will. The dark circles under his eyes screamed exhaustion. Will told his dad, "I am so tired. You're gonna have to stop texting me all night long."

Wielding words like a chef's knife, Mac sliced and diced William over and over and over. Mac seared. "Quit your belly aching. You can sleep when I'm dead." Mac attacked Will's degree choice in architecture, and even though only 20% of all college graduates landed jobs in 2009, Mac did not let up. He never cut his son any slack. "You needed a business degree. You'll never amount to anything."

I never understood how Mac justified paying for a college degree in dance for Luba and a degree in French for his wife. Tatyana spouted, "French is the language of love." Mac knew Spanish and texting.

In the afternoon on September 24, 2013, I got the call.

"Mom..."

"Will, are you okay?" A knowing fell over me. The shakiness in my son's voice told me that death had come for his father.

"Mom, Dad passed. I'm sorry, Mom. I know it's your birthday."

"No worries. I am so sorry, honey. Do you need me to come over? Are you alone?"

"No. I'm okay. Dad's minister is with me. I need to go. It's a bit surreal right now. I'll call you later."

Of all the days for Mac to die—my birthday. I thought a lot about the why of this day. I wondered if Will might hate my future birthdays, for the date now shared Mac's death anniversary. I wondered if maybe I caused his death.

Undoubtedly, God answered the prayers only God knew I prayed. "Lord please take care of William. I know Mac is going to die. Could you take him before Will is in a car accident driving hours to and from work, day after day exhausted?" Time and friends helped me come to grips with this scenario.

Will happened to be mowing at the farm when Tatyana called him, her accent even thicker than usual as she told him "I think Bill is dead."

Will went to the house. He and Mac's minister took care of necessities. I learned the value of texting during this time. Will shared thoughts and events through the written word with total privacy and freedom from listening ears. He also looked at his dad's last text messages. Bill sent an alarming text to his wife right before he died.

"Help, I need help."

She replied, "How bad is it?"

He never texted back. She kept shopping.

Chapter 37:

Endings Beget Beginnings

M ac had wrestled with cancer for ten years. Death snatched his life as we all knew it would. The element of surprise showed up anyway. I struggled with the ill-omened coincidence of the date of his death until my crazy friend Elizabeth called from Atlanta. "Gee, I am so sorry to hear Mac died. And on your birthday. If that's doesn't beat all." Her sympathetic tone switched to the mischievous, witty, and whimsical. "Gotta give it to the man, has to be the best birthday gift he ever gave you."

Some friends love you. Some friends make memories like no other. Elizabeth and I had taught nursing together at a community college. After one tense faculty meeting, we walked to our cars together. On the way, I asked, "How does a nurse educator get fired?"

"Oh, you know."

I shook my head at her. "Elizabeth, I don't know. A nurse on the floor gets fired for neglect, harm, or substance abuse. Nurse educators, I'm clueless."

"Donna, you know."

I sighed, "Elizabeth, if I knew I wouldn't be asking."

Tossing her hands high she grinned. "You sleep with a student." And we both stood in the parking lot of the college cackling.

Her call to say she knew Mac died set the stage to lighten my load of concern once again. She masterfully shot humor into a potential state of distress. Mac dying on my birthday now elicits automatic smiles from me. But I wondered about Will.

When he lost his Nana and Gaga, I never saw him cry— not in public and not in private. Maybe with this loss the faucet of grief would flow freely. I wanted to be there if he needed me. I called him the evening of Mac's death. "Will, I have two nursing conferences to attend back-to-back, one in Nashville then one in Orlando. I'm happy to cancel if you need me."

Without hesitation he said, "No Mom, you'll just make me cry. I don't know how you do it, but you do. You need to work in Hollywood with actors and actresses and direct cry scenes. Go to your conferences and don't cancel a thing. I'll be all right."

The next day Will stood calmly in my family room, looking out the bay window as woodpeckers, finches, and sparrows flit about on the bird-feeders. I fussed through my purse, hunting for my keys and debit card. We had made plans to go to lunch at the deli and order food for after the funeral. Will turned to me and said, "You know Mom, now that I think about it, I really would like you to come to the funeral. People will be there who love you and they will want to see you."

I stopped rummaging and looked up. "What day and time did you and the Russian schedule the funeral?"

"Monday at 10:00 a.m. Afterward, people will meet at the house. You can help me with that. Call Darlene, my piano teacher, and see if she can come play the grand in the parlor."

Looking at my calendar, I said, "God is amazing. I get home from Nashville on Sunday night and leave for Florida at midnight on Monday. I'll be home."

The day of the funeral came quickly. Will's organizational skills shined, and the weather cooperated. I arrived early enough at the historic McCutchanville church to visit with my friends and family members. Memories flooded my mind. Mac and I had married here, and I taught Sunday school here for many years. I took my seat in the last pew closest to the door.

Will looked sharp in his suit and tie as he walked to the podium to present a reading. "Dad wanted me to read a poem to you. It's called "This Old Clay House." I'm not even sure this is the right version, and I don't know if I can get through it." Taking his cell phone from his pocket he held it up. "Dad's been texting me a lot lately. I think he's going to text me and tell me what heaven is like. I know exactly what he's going to say. 'William, your mother was right. Aunt Bettye's not here.'"

Like an orchestra playing on cue, the church erupted with snorts, chuckles, giggles, roars, wheezes, and snickers in every key. Heads turned my way. Once people spotted me, they laughed even harder while I blushed.

Will began to read the poem and, as he predicted, got choked up. His eyes welled up and he stopped. Aching, he said, "Guys, it sure would help me right now if you all could laugh again." And the congregation laughed, and Will did, too.

I scurried to the house afterward to help and skipped the graveside service. Will's closest friends dressed in white and black came to the house, too, complete with servant hearts. They took over the kitchen, laid out the food, and served beverages. When the afternoon ended, they stayed and cleaned.

Time passed. We cracked the spine on a new chapter in the book of life. Nearly one month after Mac's death, I viewed a different Will—clear eyes, no dark circles, the picture of rest and health.

One-night Will came over for supper. While we ate, I got snarky. "Hey Will, I think your dad was a prophet. He said you could sleep when he's dead. You're sleeping really well these days, aren't you?"

"Yes, Mom, I am. And to be honest, I'm glad he's dead."

And I quietly enjoyed the shared sense of peace and relief.

Chapter 38:

Letter Art

D eath resurrects memories. The nasty ones, like thick early morning fog, obscure any glimpses of the good ones. Yet the process of sorting through a dead person's belongings may soften the sting of nasty past abuses and misconceptions. At least it did for me. As I went through my own memories, I read emails and found handwritten letters from both Mac and Gram.

Writing letters seems to be an old-fashioned art—label me a collector. I recently sifted through my box of letters, with postmarks from Arizona, Illinois, Indiana, Michigan, North Carolina, Pennsylvania, and New Mexico. I encountered a bounty of love, thanks, and encouragement from patients and their families, from students, and from co-workers that sustained me for years—1976 through 2023 to be exact. Cards from my church family and Christian retreats along with pictures kept me, so I kept them.

Letters lift fog like sunshine at dawn, exposing new light on dark days of the past.

Mac's letter said:

"Dear Donna and Allen,

Thank you for taking care of William when I was not able to."

Allen and I cared about Mac out of love and concern for William. We kept up a relationship with a broken narcissistic alcoholic. Funny how cancer can be a friend to planners. Mac planned his funeral, selected his music, his poem, and his pall bearers. Thinking about his planning reminded me of a church friend who worked in a funeral home. One day he spied Allen's truck and tucked a business card under the windshield wiper. A scribbled note on the back of the card read, "Allen, I will be the last friend who will ever let you down." A bit of humor and a bit of truth for Mac considered Allen his friend. He asked him to be a pall bearer and he was.

Mac was a multi-millionaire with loving parents, a successful banking career, and a marvelous son, and he let the devil in a bottle take him out. Few people know heavy drinking promotes cancer. Mac stayed sober for seven years, became a sponsor for others, and apologized. We accepted his apology and chose forgiveness. As he said, he was not able. We lived this sad reality.

Gram's letter shined a light on my misconceptions and harsh judgement of Jerry, the slow driving guy. While she battled with heart failure, diet changes, and loss of endurance, she wrote, "Jerry is so good to help me. He is like a woman. He can cook, clean the house, and sure helps me. I loved your Grandad you know and still do, but Donna you know I am very glad for Gerald's life with me." I cried when I read that. God knew Gram needed help after Grandpa died, so He provided the right man. And I realized a man's character can never be measured by the speedometer.

A snowball effect happens with honest self-reflection. I thought of another person I had misjudged, the custody hearing judge, and a person I truly needed to thank, Grandpa. If they were alive today, I'd mail these letters quickly.

Your Honor,

Nearly fifty years ago a fractured family with three children (my brother, little sister, and I) relied upon you to appoint responsible custodians. The behavior of my parents quickly removed them from your list of potential choices. I am so sorry you witnessed two broken people on their worst day.

To be honest I hardly recognized them as they slung snide, slippery words out of their anger-soaked, contorted faces. Seems we all disrespected your courtroom and your position as the war of our world came to a climax. I guess that is why such proceedings claim the title of custody battle.

I believe our family feud to be only one of many in your portfolio. I imagine disgruntled parents and children fill your mailbox with hate mail that keeps the shredder fed. This letter, though overdue, is one you may choose to keep.

Truth is truth regardless of where it lands on any life timeline. Your Honor you deserve to know the truth. In my brokenness and ignorance, I judged you harshly. But you did right by me. You did have exceptional sensitivity and eagle eyes at a time when I was blinded by tears and fears. I did not have a voice in the courtroom that day so long ago, but I do now.

Thank you for placing me with my grandparents. My life is rich with blessings because of your choice.

With a grateful heart,

Dr. Donna

Dear Grandpa,

During the five years I lived with you and Gram, you meant so much to me. I'll never forget when we sat cross-legged on the olive-green carpet in the living room. You held my social security card and said, "know this number just like you know your name." I recited it at least fifty times. Whenever I write it or say it, I remember you.

One Christmas I came to visit and you met me in the driveway before I even took my suitcase into the house.

"Get your boots on."

So, I did. Trekking through a foot and a half of Pennsylvania snow over half a mile through the woods, we came upon a cluster of five-foot pines.

"Pick out any one of these three."

Finally, a real tree instead of the artificial imposter. I burst with joy.

Looking back on that day I marvel. How did you know I wanted a real tree? Oh, maybe you did too? You made it happen, however, Gram always stood firm on the premise that a real tree makes a mess. Gram's prophecy came true.

Trimming the once-in-a-lifetime tree made an uncleanable, unforgiveable mess. How old were those big bulbs anyway? Burned little brown spots on that carpet. We shared Gram's Glare. I am still laughing. I felt safe with you, even in the doghouse.

I drove from Indiana to attend your fiftieth wedding anniversary. During that trip I learned why you knew me better than anyone.

Despite the clatter and chatter in the kitchen of the Grange Hall and the cleanup crew grabbing our desert dishes and clearing our table, you did something I had only witnessed once before in our lives. You cried.

Sandwiched between your red-headed twin sisters, Mae and Della, and the youngest, Nellie, stories of homelife and childhood memories managed to pour pain out of your soul. Your honest transparency hit us all with disbelief.

"I always felt like I wasn't wanted. I missed out on so much," wiping streams of sorrow from your eyes and nose with a white napkin. The girls piped up quick.

Mae said, "But you had so much love. You were so lucky. We always loved you, Merv. It was not that you were not wanted. Mom and Dad loved you so, we all did and still do."

Bewildered, I stared quietly at the scene before me. Aunt Mae later explained. "Your Grandad and the newborn baby brother went to spend time with Mom's parents after her twelfth delivery." (With ten children still at home, I wondered if true rest was possible.) Mae continued: "However, when the time came to bring the boys home, our grandparents made a request of Mom and Dad. 'We've fallen in love with Mervin and you have so many children. Could we keep him?' And our parents let him go."

Grandpa, we shared parallel lives. Growing up feeling unwanted is like running in the desert yearning for a drink from the family fountain of belonging. It must have been terribly hard for you being an only child, yet one of twelve. Maybe you spent time with your family during the holidays, kind of like visitation?

You never talked much about your mom and dad, nor your grandparents. You need to know they raised you well, they all did. They must have loved you deeply, for you loved people. God prepared you to raise me by giving you and I an identical twin-some growing up experience.

Of all the people in my life, I know without a doubt, you loved me. Your words had weight and your consistent actions added meaning. Being raised by grandparents is a blessing, I believe the blessing to be mutual. If you were still alive, I believe you would agree.

The only other time I ever saw you cry was when little sis and I bought you a statue for your birthday. You opened the top of the box and all you could see were big, bulging eyes of a guy. Pulling him up out of the box, arms behind his back, looking rather sheepish, he stood on an ivory-colored platform engraved in black, "Grandpa, you're the greatest."

Your voice cracked a muttered "Thanks" and you took off to the bedroom. In that moment I knew, you knew, I loved you too.

Love you forever,

Donna

P.S. Little sis still has your statue.

Chapter 39:

Choosing Change

L ife is like nursing exams. All questions posed are multiple choice. Whenever I take an exam, I remember the questions I answered wrong more clearly and longer than any right answers. Maybe this is normal.

It seems odd, but I tend to do the same with memories, especially when I feel people have abused or wronged me. As clear as a sunny day, I can replay bad memories complete with verbiage and emotional twang. Holding on to such an unhealthy practice causes a gut-wrenching feeling I call churn. I hate that feeling.

Years ago, I chose to change, and the catalyst came from a discussion after a Bible study session at my church. Each Thursday night our study ended with snacks and sharing prayer concerns. The group awaited Jean's request. She said, "I don't have any prayer concern. My life is perfect."

A moment of silence fell over us. Most of us leaned back in our chairs. This kind woman meant nothing arrogant or boastful. She simply smiled and explained that God's blessings provided good fortune and a healthy and happy family. No one knew how this jolted me.

On the way home I reviewed the "Ds" of my imperfect life. Divorce. Disappointment, Displacement. Dysfunction. Drinking. Death of so many family members. I wondered crazy things and ping-ponged the impossible—redesigning my life. I played "what if."

What if Mom and Dad hadn't divorced and my dream to dance had turned into reality? I could have been a prima ballerina or a Rockette. What if my life with Gram and Grandpa never happened? I doubt the ability to cook, bake, or garden jumps on the DNA strand as a strong genetic trait. I gained kitchen and garden skills side-by-side with expert mentors. And what about my grandparents?

Gram and Grandpa chose Christ because of a divorce decree. It was ironic how God used an innocent family man to save the very ones who hated him. Would they be in heaven right now if they had never gone to church or read their Bibles? What about singing? Would Grandpa have sung in a choir, or ever sung at all?

I thought of my marriage to an alcoholic millionaire. My choice. If I had never married Mac, Will wouldn't be here. And I contemplated the blessings of my less than perfect life.

Like the main character of *It's a Wonderful Life*, I experienced a Jimmy Stewart moment. Truth hit me. The life God gave me, made me. Jesus saved my soul and nursing made me whole.

And I am thankful for my less than perfect life. My choice is to live like a person who is loved, for I know that I am.

Chapter 40:

My Voice, My Choice

A buse is real. Abusers can attack any one of us, at any time and at any age. Categories designate abuse as physical, sexual, emotional, verbal, and narcissistic. Regardless of the type, they all share some degree of innocence violated, hopes and dreams smashed, and wounds in need of healing.

Everyone's story is unique. Ways to flip pain to peace differ from person to person. Here are three of the many things that made a difference in my life: seeking counseling and knowledge, redefining family, and believing God.

Proverbs 12:15 tells us "The way of a fool is right in his own eyes, but he who heeds counsel is wise." Before Allen and I married, we met with Freddie for compatibility testing. During his review of the results he said, "There is so much good here." He knew his craft. We've been together over twenty years. Please know that seeking out counseling is never a sign of weakness, but a sign of strength. Excellent counseling will include an educational element to help identify abusive behaviors, establish boundaries, develop self-care goals, and find a loving support family.

My Sunday School class watched a series by Gary Thomas titled *When to Walk Away*, which presents a much-needed healthy Christian perspective that utilizes case studies to showcase the differences between toxic and difficult people. Using Jesus as an example, viewers receive permission to walk away from abusive people. This is a key point—Jesus walked away over 40 times, and when people walked away from Him, He never chased them down, nor tossed guilt or shame on their choice.

Sometimes when we cut the cord of a family abuser, other family members cut communication lines without explanation. Here's a tip from communication theory: no communication is also communication. If someone walks away from me, I don't despair. I consider this: if their life is easier without me in it, I'm okay. I am not a perfect person, nor will I ever be. And yes, it is possible some view me as toxic, so they walk away. Out of love and respect for their choices, I won't run after them.

Redefining family requires a sincere look at the relationships in your life. Consider the vast number of people who have taught and mentored you in whatever your profession or career may be. Flip through a mental photo album of friends who supported and loved you in your life. If only we had some way to capture all the verbal thanks given freely on a daily basis, no storage space could hold them! We can add to that stockpile and be a giver as well as a receiver of love and gratitude.

Any nurse or healthcare worker can recall thanks from patients, family and co-workers. Remember when you saved a life and when you lost a life, and think of all the tears and hugs. If you are a nurse who feels you have no value, remember the nursing family loves you, and that love has no limit or boundary. Much like the love of God, it is everlasting.

Finally: I believe in God, Jesus Christ—God's one and only son—and the Holy Spirit, my comforter. I realize not everyone is Christian and not everyone likes Christians. As a spiritual care researcher, I am aware of the many diverse religions and am respectful to those who believe differently than I.

Have you ever considered this statement? "You can disagree with me, but please don't make me wrong." Believing in God may not be important in your life. But it is essential in mine. I don't intend to offend, so read on with an open mind as I share the foundation of my peace process.

If you seek peace, I know it can be found. Belief and faith unlocked the door for me. I believe God wrote me letters, love letters. I put His words and promises into my mind and broken heart. Here are some favorites to consider.

When sadness pounces because your parents chose a lover over you or abandoned you altogether, cling to these words from your heavenly Father. John 15:16 says "You did not choose me, but I chose you." According to Psalms 27:10, "When my father and my mother forsake me, Then the Lord will take care of me." In Hebrews 13:5-6 the Lord assures us that " I will never leave you nor forsake you." So we may boldly say: "The Lord is my helper; I will not fear. What can man do to me?"

I am loved by God. He wants a relationship with me. He knows I am not perfect, but broken. Psalm 147:3 states, "He heals the brokenhearted and binds up their wounds." When I feel no one cares, 1 Peter 5:7 recommends "Casting all your cares upon Him, for He cares for you."

I believe God. I believe the nature of God to be love. And one reason I am confident in the trustworthiness of His promises is due to His singular inability. There is one thing that it is impossible for God to do. Do you know what that is? He cannot lie (Hebrews 6:18). I'm a believer. I believe He loves you too.

We all have a voice, free will, and the ability to make healthy choices in our lives. Finding peace in life despite abusive behaviors is more than possible for all of us.

Forgive like my father did. Embrace those who care. Learn from life's lessons. Find a reason to be thankful every day. Love like God. Throw nasty memories in a sea of forgetfulness to be remembered no more. Enjoy this one and only life. Live like you're loved, because you are.

Now may "the Lord bless you and keep you; the Lord make His face to shine upon you and be gracious to you. The Lord lift up His countenance upon you, and give you peace" (Numbers 6:24-26,)

About the Author

D r. Donna D. Kincheloe is a Christian author, nurse educator, and speaker who uses the power of storytelling to help people consider new perspectives by weaving hope into their life circumstances. For forty-four years, Dr. Donna worked as a bedside nurse educator, researcher, and mentor. She contributed to a statistically significant spiritual care research project, published in the *Journal of Clinical Nursing*, and is the author of *I Never Walk the Halls Alone*. Dr. Donna is the mother of one adult son. She resides with her supportive, fun-loving husband Allen Dale in Evansville, Indiana.

A free ebook edition is available with the purchase of this book.

To claim your free ebook edition:

1. Visit MorganJamesBOGO.com
2. Sign your name CLEARLY in the space
3. Complete the form and submit a photo of the entire copyright page
4. You or your friend can download the ebook to your preferred device

A **FREE** ebook edition is available for you or a friend with the purchase of this print book.

CLEARLY SIGN YOUR NAME ABOVE

Instructions to claim your free ebook edition:
1. Visit MorganJamesBOGO.com
2. Sign your name CLEARLY in the space above
3. Complete the form and submit a photo of this entire page
4. You or your friend can download the ebook to your preferred device

Print & Digital Together Forever.

Snap a photo

Free ebook

Read anywhere

Printed in the USA
CPSIA information can be obtained
at www.ICGtesting.com
JSHW081953111023
50051JS00002B/11